# The 10 Year Breakfast

## or what I learnt by eating 987 breakfasts

**By David Wimblett**

Foreword by Nigel Botterill

*Book design by*
*Richard Tomlin – The Fusion Effect*

*First Published 2014 by*
*DJW Business Systems Limited – London*
*ISBN 978-1-908314-01-7*

# Thank you

To all the people I have met over my 10 years of networking, especially those that have become great friends.

# Foreword

No matter what it is in life, there's always more to it than first meets the eye.

Nigel Botterill & David Wimblett

Whether it's the inner workings of a modern day motorcar, how and why Andy Murray has emerged as one of the world's top tennis players, what has made Apple's products so successful or, the little tricks that ensure Mary Berry's own creations never suffer from a soggy bottom, the devil is in the detail.

I've studied all these conundrums and, many more in recent times. In truth, I've built my entire business on studying the detail of successful things that other people have done.

What are the ingredients of a web page that can sell £3 million of products in under, three years?

What makes the difference between a 200% ROI and Google Ad Words and a 2,000% ROI?

I know the answers because I've studied the experts and learnt this stuff and, the experts that I turned to, were those who really knew what they were talking about, which is why you should pay attention to the book that you have in your hand right now.

You see, whilst it's (relatively!) easy to write about 987 breakfasts over ten years, the truth of it is, that's a lot of experience and learning (and eggs) – but David's done it.

What's more, by his own admission, he wasn't very good at this 'networking thing' when he first started and that makes him even more interesting and fascinating to me, because he's come from a position of incompetence and poor results, to master what he does.

Critically, his success as a networker isn't innate which has helped him to teach and share his lessons along the way in a very accessible style.

Look, let's be honest – this isn't rocket science. But David tells some interesting, and on occasions amusing, anecdotes and out of all his stories emerge a suite of lessons and reminders that will enrich you, dear reader. They won't enhance the technology in your pocket; you're not going to win a major sporting event as a result; and your baking output will be completely unaffected by what lies in the pages ahead but success when you're networking depends on the little things just the same as it does in any other aspect of life and  a rich cornucopia of devlish detail and small hinges that can swing big doors awaits you. *Enjoy…*

*Nigel Botterill*
*March 2014*

# Why this book?

Nine hundred and eighty seven breakfasts, in the main Full English, equates for me to ten years of organised networking. My book is about business; it is about what I have learnt about business whilst networking. In the main it has been as a long-time member, and director, of BNI (Business Network International), but also as a member of 4 Networking, Business Biscottii, The Best of Richmond, The Chamber of Commerce, and a number of other organisations, most recently the Entrepreneur's Circle.

My journey takes me from being the most invisible of members to a BNI Area Director known around the world (I'm pretty well known in New Zealand). I have made many friends over the years and some are mentioned in the pages that follow, while others are not, to protect both the guilty and the innocent.

My book, I hope, will help you on your own business journey and allow you to get more out of what you do and you certainly don't have to be a member of BNI, or even network, to benefit from my ten years of eating breakfasts.

Business works on all sorts of levels and in very different ways for different people, but the one, over-riding thing that I have learnt over the past ten years, is that knowing something is only a very small part of the game. Thinking is a major part, but that implementation, the actual doing, is by far the most critical part of running a truly successful business.

Even then, more importantly than just doing, is the way in which you do those things. And I especially like the way Nigel Botterill talks about this; he calls it the Bananarama Syndrome. 'It ain't what you do, it's the way that you do it. And that's what gets results.'

So please enjoy the read and just make sure that you have a high lighter pen at the ready, to mark the things that you want to implement.

# An invisible member!

Things have changed a great deal during my ten years of networking and one of them is to my own personal confidence. When I joined my first networking group, I now realise that I was as quiet as a mouse, I wouldn't have said 'boo to a goose', and to be honest I was an invisible member.

Here's a little game for you, if you are a member of a networking group with a fixed membership (like BNI). Stop reading right now (well when you've finished this paragraph) and get yourself a piece of paper and a pen. Then list every member of your group – just from memory. If you find it difficult, think about what categories you have in your group; think about who does what job for your group; think about where people sit (some members always sit in the same seats). Even after all of that I wouldn't mind betting that you can't think of the names of a member or two. Well, if that's the case, those members are like I was – invisible. Obviously remembering every member in large group is much more taxing, but the principle still stands. Okay, time to give it a try.

So, how did you do? How long did it take you?

Now this is a great example of both visibility and connections. By connections I mean friends, members you get on with, and those that have related businesses to yours. I'm sure that the first ten or so members you just scribbled down one after the other, just as fast as you could write. Why? Because they are the visible members in your group and you know them well, but when you get to the last few members, the ones you really had to rack your brains to remember, well they are your invisible members and I doubt you pass more than just the time of day with. So, what's the big deal?

To answer that let's return to my membership of my group. In my first year as a member I received very few referrals and so got very little business. Why? Because no one really knew I existed (my fault) and so never thought about me outside of the meetings. I just didn't make an impression. But then I became the Chapter Director (an interesting outcome for an invisible member) and things changed. I had all of a sudden become visible.

As Chapter Director my confidence grew more and more each week - not that I really noticed at the time - and it wasn't long before I felt comfortable in the role. People seemed to like my leadership and the direction I was taking the group, so much so that I stayed on for a second term of office. I guess I knew that I was growing as a person, but it wasn't until a friend of mine, who knew me before networking (and had been out of the country for some years), visited the group one morning, that it really sunk in. She said that she was amazed at how different I was 'no longer the shy man she used to know'. I have to say it surprised me.

Now I'm sure that you have heard of VCP. It stands for visibility, credibility and profitability. Well I was now visible, it also seems that I was credible, and the referrals had begun to flow. I can safely say, with the benefit of hindsight, that becoming a Chapter Director was one of the smartest moves I've ever made.

But there are drawbacks and things to remember about being visible. I've met so many people that think being visible is all they need to do, and then all the business they want will follow.

Maybe it's because of the way leadership positions in the various groups are 'sold' – for example, 'be the group leader as it will give you more visibility', with the inference that you will also get more referrals. And to a degree, of course, that is true. But it misses out a very important step - credibility. Because it doesn't matter how visible you are, unless you are credible, referrals will not follow.

I can remember a member; a big man, with a big voice, and an enormous personality. As soon as he walked in the room, everyone knew he had arrived (he would be the first person you wrote on your list of members), but he didn't get that many referrals. Why? Because he hadn't built the credibility that went with his visibility.

There was also a lady I remember, she was fairly visible and received a reasonably good number of referrals. But then she joined the Leadership Team of her group and, to be frank, she was pretty poor at the job. The problem was that by being unreliable and disorganised, and being visible, so that all the members could see what she was really like, affected the number of referrals she was given. It was very sad and, although she was offered help, she ended up leaving the group.

So, if you are networking, part of a business group, the first thing you have to do is to become visible. But then the hard work starts. Imagine that you have just paid for a half-page advert in the perfect magazine for your business. At the top of your advert is your company name. However, the remainder of the advert is just blank. Well that's exactly what you are like when you first start networking. But, and here's the big difference, no one would dream of running a blank advert, but lots of people run 'blank adverts' when they network.

In some ways credibility is just like marketing, building the content for your advert. What will your advert look like (personal presentation)? What do you do? How do you help us? What are you offering? How do we contact you? What proof is there that you are any good (testimonials)? You would fill the full half-page of your advert, and so you must when you go networking.

But, the great thing that an advert can't do but you can, is build credibility in so many other ways, and this is what is missed by a great many, in fact too many, business people.

Obviously you must demonstrate that you are good at your job, but there's so much more to being credible than just being good at what you do. Are you reliable? For example: come to meetings, arrive on time, do things when you say you are going to. Are you the sort of person that others would like to help run their group? Are you organised? Are you a leader, or do you leave it to others to do the work? Do you go out of your way to help people? Are you positive? Are you passionate about what you do? Does what you say, and do, 'stack up'? Are you the sort of person that you would want to do business with?

Credibility is so important, but as with being visible, there's no point unless you are credible. Being credible won't do you much good if you are invisible (as I discovered).

So, you must be both visible and credible, and then sell your business well, in order to reap the rewards of profitability.

# A lovely glass of wine...

I don't know when mass networking started, as we know it today, organised meetings with food and drinks, but I do know that I hadn't done much networking until about ten years ago. Today you can network over breakfast, lunch, dinner, evening and, of course, online. There are hundreds of events and almost as many variations of group; from one-off occasions to structured weekly meetings. But they all have one thing in common and that is that most people that network gain very little from the time they spend networking.

I could write a whole book just on networking (perhaps I will), as it's a subject that I have presented on many times, plus I have attended hundreds of networking events, but for now I'm just going to tell a story or two that I hope will help you get a great deal more out of the networking you do, and help you achieve some truly worthwhile results.

My first attempts at networking were, I suspect, like many other people's when analysed: pretty much a waste of my time. If I was lucky I went home with a few business cards in my pocket, new contacts, having given out some of my own cards. My cards were now in other people's pockets, new contacts, but in reality they were the same contacts, as most people when networking just exchange cards.

Normally, the evening would start with a glass of wine and a trip to the food table, as I was missing my dinner at home. Often, my evening would also end at the food table because having eaten all I could and having found no one to talk to I went home. I did, on occasion, exchange pleasantries, between mouthfuls of food, on the quality of the banquet, with other poor souls suffering the same ordeal. But that was about it.

I did in fact dread people wanting to introduce themselves because with a full plate of food in one hand and a glass and a fork in the other hand, things were a little tricky. Shaking hands became an embarrassing ritual, often ending up with a sort of back-of-hand bump.

I found it easier with women as many didn't like to shake hands anyway and instead just smiled. I could do that; well, almost!

Things had to change if I was going to get anything worthwhile out of my networking, and so I decided to improve my networking skills. The first part was easy; don't eat and drink at the same time. The second was a little more difficult, leaving the comfort of the food table behind. I would no longer be able to consider the merits of an egg sandwich over a mini pork pie to avoid having to speak with someone passing close by.

So, I was now free in the room, ready to network, a glass in one hand and the other ready to shake any hand that came close enough. However, very few hands were offered. My new tactic wasn't working and now I was completely exposed just wandering around the room. I felt the need for another mini pork pie.

I needed a plan; there was more to this networking lark than I had thought. Much more.

By now I had attended a number of networking events and had got used to being in a room with 50, sometimes over 100, people all talking at once (well hopefully only half of them). All trying to make themselves heard over all the other people trying to make themselves heard. Being a quiet kind of bloke this took some getting used to I can tell you. At first I just listened; well, tried to.

And this was when my break-through to worthwhile networking happened. I spotted a lady, all on her own, who to be honest looked shell-shocked. This was the time for a knight in shining armour. Well okay, a man with a glass of chardonnay.

I crossed the room, smiled at her, introduced myself, offered her the glass of wine, which she happily took, and asked her name. And then I asked her the big one, "Your first time?" She nodded and added that she had no idea what to do. It was so packed and so noisy.

This was my chance to share with her three of the most important things about networking that I had learnt. Firstly, the evening was not about selling her services, as most of the people in the room were not buying. But, even if they were, what were the chances of them wanting to buy what she was selling exactly at that moment? In truth, very little. Obviously it happens now and again, but then occasionally, so do long shots win the Derby.

So I explained that networking was nothing to do with selling but instead all about starting a relationship, and so networking was all about arranging a meeting at a future date. Having a cup of coffee to find out how they could help each other.

Secondly, she must have a plan. Not like my first efforts at networking where my only goal was to get some food and a drink and survive the evening. It didn't have to be anything major but, on the other hand, far better than collecting a pocket full of business cards. I suggested that three meetings at a later date was a pretty good goal.

And finally, what to talk about. Not you for starters. No-one enjoys having a business card thrust in their face and then being told by the person everything they do for the next twenty, minutes.

I advised her to ask about the other person, as most people are comfortable about talking about themselves. And that her questions didn't have to be the sort of thing you heard on Mastermind, but on the other hand slightly better than "Did you come by car?"

I also suggested that instead of asking people what they did, because often when they tell you all you can say is "Oh" or "That's interesting", to ask instead how they help people. Because you will get a much more interesting reply. After all, ask an accountant what they do and the standard reply will be, is "I'm an accountant", (Sorry if you are an accountant and you never answer that way). But ask the same accountant how they help people, and for one thing they can't say "I'm an accountant" which is a great start, but they could say just about anything else. Like, "I get the taxman to pay for your holidays". You've got to admit that you would have to ask how.

One of the things I like to find out is what the person is aiming to get out of the event; are they looking to meet someone in particular? I may be able to help them and more, I'm showing them from the very beginning of our relationship that I'm interested in them. It's not all about me.

So, having conveyed my pearls of wisdom we said our goodbyes and I wished her luck with the rest of the evening.

First thing the next morning (she had asked for my business card) I had an email from her saying how much she enjoyed chatting with me and that without my guidance she may never have gone networking again. As it was, she had followed my advice and did indeed have three meetings lined up the following week.

For me the great thing was that from that event on I followed my own advice and, I have to say, that it has been very effective.

Note: *I have kept in touch with the lady ever since and we are still friends today.*

# Caught on film!

"David. Come on, your turn."

For a moment I just sat and hoped that I was hiding my shock. I was thinking 'You must be joking', amongst other things – like how could I get out of this?

I was at a special, one-off Presentation Skills workshop. I was there because a good friend of mine had asked me to come along and tell him what I thought of his idea. Until this moment I had been sitting at the back of the room observing, minding my own business. Now my friend was beaming at me and signalling for me to join him at the front of the room. At that moment I hated him!

Now you might be thinking that this is a little extreme, but let me explain.

The workshop was special because those present – the numbers were limited – were going to be filmed, from a script they had prepared, then critiqued by a lady BBC Television presenter (a friend of my friend), and then filmed again. A brilliant idea. And, as I say, I had been asked along just to give some feedback. I hadn't known what was going on before I had arrived, didn't expect to be filmed, and of course hadn't prepared, let alone practised, a script. To some degree, none of that really matter. What did, was that I was the person who normally ran the Presentation Skills workshops for the people in the room. There-fore, I had to be good if I were to keep any kind of credibility.

And at that moment everyone was looking at me, waiting for me to move.

I looked at my friend's smiling face and said, "Of course. I'd love to."

In the few seconds that it took to reach the front of the room I had to think of a topic and be ready to present. The camera man said that he was 'rolling' and I could start whenever I was ready. I nodded to him and was off. The amazing thing? I was pretty spot-on with my timing. But what was really worrying me was the critique to follow.

The videos were replayed and the lady from the BBC advised on both content and presentation. She pointed out the good things and how the not-so-good things could be improved. When it was my turn for her critique, all I could think was that it was too late. I'd been caught on film. As it turned out, I have to say that she was very kind to me, and said that the only improvement she could suggest was for me to wear a coloured shirt, not a white one. I have to admit that I was a little disappointed that there wasn't more. However, my reputation was intact. (The actual video shot of my presentation can be seen on my YouTube Channel – see below).

The evening turned out to be a real success and all of those present learned a great deal.

I really recommend that you get yourself filmed presenting, as it can teach you such a lot. However, it can be a 'tough' watch, as I discovered when I was next filmed. On this occasion I was presenting for ten minutes; part of a large networking event. Watching myself for ten minutes was hard work, but I did learn a lot. It's very different from presenting for just 60 seconds. Boy did I fiddle. Stroke my nose. I had to stop all of that!

Since that first time I have made a fair number of videos and they have been used all around the world to educate people about networking. I've even had the National BNI Director from Cyprus contact me and ask if I would make a video on a subject that they needed covering. I was very pleased to do so. I think my favourite video of those I've made is one I shot for a competition. It's the only video I've done, shot with a co-star, Helen Baden. It is based on the comedy sketch, 'Alas Smith and Jones'. It's over five minutes long and Helen and I shot it in one continuous take. In the film we explain what a referral is; it's well worth a watch.

So, video is brilliant in improving your presentation skills, but today it has an even bigger role to play. In fact, so big is this role that if you don't have a video for your business you are at a distinct disadvantage. Why? Because unless you have a video on the homepage (landing page) of your website you will be losing out on traffic. Google loves video; mainly because it owns YouTube. In addition, video is a great way of driving traffic to your website in the first place. And, of course, video is a brilliant way of getting your clients, and would-be clients, to engage with your company. All of this makes video a great, and must-have, business tool.

Now I know what you're thinking. You don't know what to make a video about. You're no actor. And videos are expensive to make. And you would be wrong on all three counts.

The first problem, what to make your video about, just takes a bit of thought. A great place to start here is FAQs - Frequently Asked Questions. There must be loads of questions that your customers are always asking you; you may already have a FAQ page on your website. So turn them into video. Then of course there are 'How to...' videos. Again you have lots of choice here. Product videos are an obvious area and will give you plenty of scope. And don't forget customer testimonials; there is nothing like a real live customer telling people how good you are.

Okay, you're not an actor. I will admit that if you have a face 'better suited to radio' and you can't string more than a few words together coherently you may have a problem. But even then I think you would surprise yourself if you tried. Remember you don't have to shoot the perfect video on the first take (or even the first video). The big thing is that people buy people, real people, so just be yourself when the camera is rolling. But if you are dead set against being in front of a camera, I bet one of your staff might fancy themselves as a future film star. Or failing that how about a friend? However, if, at the end of the day, you have to hire a professional actor, again it's not as expensive as you may think, and could well be a brilliant investment.

So, we are down to cost. How much should a video cost? Well there's only one answer here, 'How long is a piece of string?' There are so many variables here that it is impossible to answer that question, so I'm not going to try. However, what I will say is that you can shoot a perfectly good video for free. These days just about every mobile phone can take video and, with a little bit of thought, you can get some very reasonable results (just don't forget the sound).

Here are a few pointers to get you started. Video length: 30 seconds to about two minutes is best. Use emotion and humour. Think about your audience first; you need to engage them in the first few seconds. Think about the videos you like. What is it about them that gets you to watch? Bet it's not the content and that it's more likely the way the content is portrayed. And finally, if you have to convince yourself that your film is okay, start again!

*On my YouTube channel:*
*BNI – Thank You for the Business and BNI – How to find a referral – ALAS BADEN and WIMBLETT*

# Turning Japanese

In 1980, The Vapors released a song called Turning Japanese. It seems so long ago, but thirty odd years later I still love the song. I just really like the chorus line "I think I'm turning Japanese, I really think so". Well, in 2007 I was invited to Tokyo by my good friend Asato Ohno, the National Director of BNI in Japan. Asato and I had first met when we were both members of a new BNI chapter being set up by Regional Director Lawrence Dagnall in 2001 near Heathrow.

So, it was one bright morning, after a twelve hour plus flight from London, that Lawrence and I landed at Narita airport in Tokyo. Asato met us and then we were introduced to the Tokyo Metro. What an amazing spectacle: so many people, but so organised. I've never seen such patient and ordered lines of people in my life. Our schedule over the next few days was pretty full on, starting with a visit to the National Office right then, and then a New Member workshop in the evening.

I have to admit that the workshop in the evening was a bit of a struggle. Firstly, because it was spoken totally in Japanese and I don't speak a word. But secondly, because by that time I hadn't really had any sleep for over 24 hours.

However, things were pretty good, as every time I looked across at the young lady sitting opposite me she smiled at me. My embarrassment only became clear a few hours later, after the workshop, and we were on our way to our hotel, and Asato informed me that the reason the young lady was smiling at me was that I looked across at her every time I woke up. It seems that she was amused at my efforts to make it look like I wasn't sleeping the entire evening.

Still, after a good night's sleep, it was up early and off to our first breakfast meeting in Japan. I wondered if I might meet the young lady again, as I thought we had made a connection.

As a BNI Area Director, during the course of a year I would run around 30 workshops on topics such as referral skills, networking skills, and presentation skills. One of the things we discuss in the presentation skills workshop is nonverbal communication and we cite the work of Albert Mehrabian, Professor Emeritus of Psychology at UCLA. His work concluded that words only account for 7% of your message, whereas your voice accounts for 38% and your body language for 55%.

Now there has been a lot said about Professor Mehrabian's findings. However, I have to say that I wasn't totally convinced about the 7%, especially as I am a writer.

However, the next 90 minutes were going to change my thinking and prove that Professor Mehrabian was without doubt correct.

During a BNI meeting, each member of the group gets 60 Seconds to talk about their business. Usually it's a sales pitch. It's a one minute commercial and, done well, can produce brilliant results.

Anyway, back to my BNI meeting that morning. The young lady wasn't there, which thinking about it was probably just as well, as after all, what would I say? "Sorry about falling asleep yesterday evening."

There were 35 members in the group and this time I made sure that I listened intently, nodded where I thought appropriate, and even smiled. By the end of their 'commercials' I had decided that there were four people that I would like to speak to at the end of the meeting. But then the penny dropped. The whole meeting had been conducted in Japanese. I had absolutely no idea what these four people had been talking about; I just liked them. Why? Well it certainly wasn't the words they used. And, that's when I thought of Professor Mehrabian, as it had to be because of their voices and body language. Suddenly I understood far more about the results of his work. But I still felt that a little more research was needed and so turned to the internet.

There is a whole book on the subject 'Silent Messages' but, in short, the results were based on a particular subject and were for Total Liking of the person. And the full results are these: Total Liking = 7% Verbal Liking + 38% Vocal Liking + 55% Facial Liking.

Now this makes a great deal more sense and explains why I liked the four people at this BNI meeting. I liked their voices and their faces.

Why is this important and, how can it help your business?

Well, in the main, we all like to do business with friends, people we like, and even if perhaps they are not the absolute best at what they do, if we like the person, we will still do business with them. Just take a moment to think about it and you will know that it's true. It's even true of companies. If you like a company, you are more likely to give them your business.

I'm sure that as a business person you have spent time crafting your message. In some cases, you may have spent hours on some copy. But how long have you spent working on the way you will deliver those words; working on your voice and the way you look? And I don't just mean if you are giving a presentation, but every time you speak: to clients, to staff, your suppliers and when out networking.

Smiling is an easy thing, as I found in Japan. Smile at someone and they will smile back, but it's surprising how many people rarely smile. As a rule do you buy from people who are always miserable? I doubt it.

Being liked is vital to your success in business, in fact in life, and as I discovered in Japan and Professor Mehrabian has proved, the way you say what you say, and how you look while saying whatever it is, counts for far more than the actual words themselves.

# I blame it on Kevin Costner!

In 1989 Kevin Costner starred in 'Field of Dreams' in which he built a baseball diamond and the Chicago Black Sox came to play. "Build it and they will come," he was told. It's actually a very good film and a brilliant story about following your dream, even when, just about, all around you are convinced you are out of your mind and what you are doing is both a waste of time and money. It's about strength of character and a belief that what you are doing is right.

The problem is that many business owners do just the same. They start a business and expect customers just to turn up at their front door. But of course, in real life, they don't! In fact, if your dream has any chance of coming true, there is a great deal of hard work to be done first.

But, for now, back to the "Build it and they will come" trap, that many business owners fall into, and I think it's important to add here, not just new business owners.

This story, for some reason, makes me particularly sad. Maybe it's because the business was run by two lovely young ladies, maybe it's because their product was in truth very good and it was such a waste, maybe because I feel that I could have done more to help them, but whatever the reason I still feel sad when I think about it today. When I break their story down, it isn't that very different from others I have witnessed over the years; businesses which have suffered a similar fate. But for some reason it just feels different.

I actually came across the business because one of my friends suggested that I could help them with the layout of their new price list. At this stage I knew nothing about the business, other than it was a coffee shop in my local shopping centre. I arrived the next day nice and early for my appointment and was welcomed by two lovely ladies; it was their business and they had been open just three days. I was invited in and was treated to a great cup of coffee. I also discovered that they baked beautiful cakes, served very tasty lunches, and that everything was cooked in their own kitchen.

The décor was clean and modern, as yet without any real character, but what did surprise me was the size of the place. They would need a lot of customers to fill it. To me it had the feel of a large canteen.

But that wasn't their biggest problem. They were a new, unknown business, whose premises were based in a cut-through between two major parts of the town and, worse still, surrounded by well-known coffee brands. They told me that the rent was cheap, all they could afford, but obviously there was a reason for the low rent.

As we sat and drank the lovely coffee, and discussed their tiny price list, I pointed to the people passing by outside. They were all walking fast, heads down, not one glanced our way.

The trouble was that they thought that by just being open, that when people got to hear about how wonderful their coffee and food were that customers would be queuing at their door. They really believed that an open door and an 'A' Board outside their shop would be enough to have people pouring in. And of course it wasn't and they didn't.

And despite my best efforts, and staff just standing around doing nothing, they wouldn't do any effective marketing. So much could have been done, simply and cheaply.

Nothing much changed over the next few months. I would pop in every so often and sometimes it was busier than others. The coffee was still great and the food excellent, but there were never really enough customers. I would ask how their marketing was going and what offers they had introduced, but other than a loyalty card and some flimsy bits of paper on the tables there wasn't much.

A few months later I popped by for another coffee. Sadly, everything was locked up and there was an eviction notice stuck to the door. Inside everything was still there, even personal stuff. It was so sad.

Building it and hoping that customers will turn up is not a recipe for success, as these two young ladies found out.

Marketing is the most important thing you do as a business owner, no matter what type of business you run. Getting customers, and keeping them, is the key to your long term success. So, if you don't have a marketing plan, stop reading right now and write on the top of a piece of paper in large letters – My Marketing Plan. Then underneath start making your plan; it only needs to be simple for now. The most important thing is to start. Your plan may just be to buy a book on marketing. But the critical thing is to have a plan.

And, in case you haven't got the message yet, just hoping that business will turn up is not a marketing plan.

And, the other thing about marketing, it's not a 'one-off' but something you should be doing every day.

Please don't let your business suffer because having opened for business you expect your customers to find you; it's your job to help your customers to find you. There's a big difference – and one that brings major rewards.

# How smart are you?

It doesn't matter if you are part of a football team, a rowing eight, ski team, basketball team, or sailing race team; the best results come when the members of that team work together and have a common goal. And it's just the same with any networking group.

However, more often than not, it's the working together that causes the most problems. I don't think I've ever come across a group that didn't want more business. But, I've come across many groups that couldn't agree on how best to achieve it. Or, who didn't think that all of the members were doing their fair share of the work.

The thing is that every member has their own goals and abilities. And some are, just plain lazy. But what most members miss is that unless they all work together, they all lose. While they may not all work together, they certainly all lose together.

Then of course you get the members who suggest that the best person at a particular job, does that job. And I totally agree. However, I've also suffered at the hands of this idea, when it was suggested to me that I invite all the visitors to a group and let this person, and others, invite none. Not much team work going on there. Now, I accept that I was successful at finding visitors, but that didn't mean that other members didn't have to try. That was just a cop out. Obviously, I wouldn't expect them to bring as many visitors as I did, but I would expect them to bring one or two.

Now before you think I'm being un-reasonable let me give you an example. Let's think of a football team. We have eleven players, including a centre forward, who hopefully scores lots of goals, and a goalkeeper, who, with any luck, will stop lots of goals. Two very different jobs; like me getting lots of visitors and another member getting none (maybe they are great at getting referrals). But, the centre forward, will often be found helping out in defence, and, when needs must, a goalkeeper will be in the opposing team's penalty box trying to score a goal. They are a team, and they all do the very best they can. Neither the centre forward or the goalkeeper sits back and lets the other one get on with it. They win as a team, or lose as a team.

Something that works well in a serious networking group, and helps all members to participate fully, is the Six Week Resolution. It's a very simple idea and helps the whole group to work together, but also takes into account each member's personal skills. Basically, the Six Week Resolution is a set of goals for the group over a six week period. During the six weeks members commit to bringing a certain number of referrals, visitors, having One-2-Ones, and attending workshops. Each member has their own target: it must stretch them, and it must cover all four things. And there is a minimum total number overall. The idea is that every member will commit to being 'the best member they can be'.

It's a wonderful incentive for a group, works really well, and means that everyone can really get involved as it is run over six weeks. The Six Week Resolution also has an added benefit, when you add up the total target, for all of the members, it is often a lot higher than a group would have set for themselves as a whole.

The reason that the Six Week Resolution works so well is that it is a SMART goal. Every member is working for the team (group) but they have set their own goals which are; Specific, Measurable, Attainable, Realistic and Timely (the time being the only one set by the group) to themselves. So they believe in them and, therefore, have a far greater chance of success.

Okay, some members will have small goals, while others will have large goals, and, yes, some members will still try and take it easy. But overall the Six Week Resolution is a great way of getting a group working together. Often this continues long after the six weeks has passed because of the success they have all become accustomed to.

Now I suggest that you have a large goal; think big. Man would never have got to the moon without a rather large goal.

But, a word of warning. Remember that a goal needs to be Smart and you should also take into consideration what you do.

I was at a group once and it was the first meeting of the New Year. The members had been asked to come back after Christmas with their personal goals, for the chapter, for the coming year. I have to say that there were some very good goals. Then the business coach got up. One of his goals was to bring 50 visitors to the group during the year. Up until that point he hadn't brought a single visitor to a meeting. There was nothing Smart about his goal and sadly he didn't achieve it. Now missing a goal is not a bad thing. As if you aim for fifty visitors and you only bring forty, well, frankly that is amazing. But bring just four visitors, and that's another story.

As a business coach his credibility was shot. Would you have let him advise you on setting your goals? Somehow, I doubt it. And that means you wouldn't refer him either.

# Here, there, everywhere!

In 2005, Nick Taimitarha started The Best of Richmond and in the December of that year he joined the Tudor chapter of BNI (Business Network International) based in Hampton Hill. That is where we first met.

Nick is one of those people you just can't help but like; he will always help you if he can, and he is very easy to work with. So it wasn't long before I found myself helping him find businesses to join the Best of Richmond.

The offering really was a bit of a 'No Brainer', as it still is today, for the best local businesses looking for a worthwhile online presence. In particular, it was a brilliant way for businesses without their own website to get online and be, in effect, on the first page of Google.

In those early days, in fact for a number of years, it didn't matter where I went in Teddington, Twickenham and Richmond, Nick was always there. He must have spent almost all of every day on the road meeting local business owners. He was doing the hard work; the stuff that really matters.

And so it's no surprise that Nick has been one of the top 'thebestof' franchisees in the UK for many years.

Nick also runs some really successful networking events, often with over 100 people attending, and his riverboat networking events on the Thames, with Turk Launches, are a highlight of the summer.

A few years after I met Nick another person who had purchased an online directory franchise, City Local, also joined a nearby BNI chapter. Obviously following someone else, especially if that person is very successful, is difficult, but no way impossible. So when I was asked how they could make a success of their business, amongst other things, I suggested that they model themselves on Nick, with regard to work ethic and doing the right things.

The trouble was this person never did. Instead they spent hours, I won't say working, on their laptop. I often wondered what they did all day (including Saturdays) when they had so few customers. Further, we even talked about them holding events so that local business owners got to know the brand, not a copy of 'thebestof' events, something different, but these never happened either.

To my mind this was a classic case of being a master at getting ready. Creating the perfect welcome letter, an Excel sheet of projected earnings, record sheets for this and that, a third, if not fourth, new business card design.

In fact anything to avoid having to do the things that really matter, the things that would help make a successful business. Put simply – make sales.

Sadly, about 18 months later, the person gave up on the franchise as he had run out of money. Now there may have been other considerations and reasons behind this decision to quit, but had the business had lots of customers and been making good money I know it would have been a different one.

So, why did he avoid the 'selling'? The same reason we all do. Because, let's face it, at some time, we have all done it. Avoided doing what we know needs to be done. And I'm not just talking about making sales here. It can be anything. Calling a difficult client, opening a letter that we know is trouble, speaking to a member of staff about their time-keeping, the list is endless. And so are the reasons not to do whatever it is. We can convince ourselves of just about anything if we really want to. Sorting out the in-tray is certainly more important than calling a potential new client, if we want it to be. Our rationale? They probably won't want to speak to us any way; so it's a waste of time.

So, why do we all do this?

Well, the list is long, and whole books have been written on the subject, but here are a few reasons:
1) Habit – we just put things off.
2) Fear of failure – so we don't start. If we don't start some thing, we can't fail. But in actual fact not starting something is in itself failure. I've discovered that one to my cost.
3) Rejection – very few of us take rejection easily. It's personal. It certainly is when you walk across the dance floor to ask a beautiful girl to dance and she says no. But, it's not when they say no to your online directory offering.
4) Waiting for the right moment – it rarely comes.
5) Needing time to think about it – the master of getting ready.
6) The job is too big – just don't know where to start.
7) Self-doubt – I'm rubbish at this.
8) Comfort Zone – we like what we know.

I'm sure that you can think off many more reasons for putting things off and I expect have your very own reason for not doing all sorts of things.

The problem is, we know we are putting things off, we might even know that if we put whatever it is off long enough, that it may come back and 'bite' us, but we still do it. Why? Because we convince ourselves that if we put off whatever it is the 'pain' may never come; it's in the future. Not here, right now.

So how can we get over the problem? Well here are a few things that I have learnt can help:

1) Have a plan – most people don't. So of course they can't fail.

2) Eliminate distractions – could be as simple as turning off your phone. Or not going into the office first thing in the morning.

3) Reward yourself – just simple little things. I once had a target for appointments when Cold-Calling. I could stop when I had made my daily appointment – whether it was on the first call or the forty-first.

4) Problem too big – most things can be broken down into bite-sized chunks. Need fifty new clients this year? Don't focus on the fifty new clients, focus instead on one new client this week.

5) Motivation – if you can't motivate yourself, or have any one who can, find yourself a great mentor.

One thing I have found that makes the biggest difference is to have a compelling reason. Not, well it would be nice to. But a really compelling reason; one you would almost die for.

Nick had a compelling reason; he had to replace a very good income fast. He was also given some sage advice, as he was told that for a while "he would have to become the busiest man in Britain", if he were to fulfil his goal.

I've met hundreds of people over the past ten years and when I've asked why they do what they do, it's something like: well I couldn't work for anyone, I want to earn lots of money, to have more free time, and so on. But why? What's the compelling reason? Why do you want more money? More free time? What are you going to do with it? What is going to make you jump out of bed in the morning when all you have to do that day is a load of stuff you don't want to do?

Really understand your compelling reason, in fact find your compelling reason, and there is a real chance that you will achieve what you are looking for.

# How deep will you go?

As I've already said, visitors are the life-blood of any networking (referral) group, as without them a group will eventually fail. Why? Because a networking group is like every other business. Unless it is growing, it is shrinking. There's no such thing as standing still.

The only trouble with visitors is, as BNI says, a networking group can work for any business but not every person. Now the reasons as to why this is so are varied and almost limitless but one of them is, at the very least, short-sighted and at the worst arrogant. Or, maybe, to be fair, just ignorant. Several years ago I remember this one visitor. Our group had a very good meeting with five visitors and our BNI Area Director attending. Pretty good, even if I say so myself. After the meeting the visitors are invited to a Q&A and asked if they would like to apply to join the group.

During the Q&A, everything about being a member of BNI and the group is explained, and then the person running the session, this time our Area Director, answers any questions that might arise. Mostly the questions are pretty standard: concerns over attendance and what a substitute is, contributing each week, category limitations, and the like.

That day one person, a man, just sat through the Q&A without saying a word. Nor did he ask any questions. Sometimes it's like that, the person knows it's not for them, so they just politely sit and listen.

At this time the Area Director was Dinah Liversidge. She was an excellent director and we had worked together for a number of years. As the man left, she thanked him for attending, said that she hoped he had got something from the meeting, and could she ask why he didn't think the group would work for him?

He explained that he had studied the list of members and most of them were small businesses and tradesmen. None of them were the level of business he required; they were all too small. Dinah reminded him that the members in the room were not prospective customers, they were like his sales and marketing department, and, as he got to know them, they would introduce him to their contacts. His reply was that no one in the group would know the sort of people he wanted to know. I'm going for both short-sighted and arrogant now; maybe even ignorant as well.

Out of interest, Dinah asked, if he could give her an idea of the sort of business he was looking for. His reply, big ones, like GlaxoSmithKline. And with that he left.

Now had he bothered to find out, this man would have discovered that he had been talking to the very person he wanted to meet, because Dinah had been the International Event Manager for GSK for many years in the nineties. Running their event programme for the entire GSK product range, world-wide. What a missed opportunity!

The thing is that far too many people confuse the size of their network with success. It's just the same with databases, 'Likes' on Facebook and 'Followers' on Twitter. Numbers in themselves don't matter, it's the relationship with those people that actually matters. The problem is it takes time and effort to build a relationship, so instead, poor networkers spend their time visiting every networking group they can, hoping that one day their perfect client will drop into their lap. Of course it seldom does. It's the same with some people who join networking groups; they get very little instant business and so after a few months leave.

It's madness!

Successful networking is about the depth of your network, your relationships, and not its size. If you are a member of a networking group you may be into your second year of membership before you start to see truly good results. It's the depth that is the real key; how deep you are prepared to go, to build those relationships. And a great place to start is to look a little further than what you see directly in front of you. That lady who runs a small roofing company may have just, a few years earlier, worked for GSK.

One of my favourite questions to ask the people I meet is what they were doing ten years ago. Believe me you get some very interesting and surprising answers and it can make a big difference to your relationship and the contacts you make.

Rather different to a Will Writer I overheard once at a Networking event. I promise you that this is no word of a lie. He approached this unfortunate person, introduced himself, and then asked the person if they had a will. I confess that what the person said surprised me. Because he said, "Yes."

Just in case you don't know, only around thirty percent of the population have a will. But that didn't surprise me anywhere as much as what the Will Writer said and did next. "Well, you're no good to me!" and with that walked off, leaving his victim doing a good impression of a goldfish.

It was just another example of poor, in fact very bad, networking. Imagine what might have happened if the Will Writer had taken the time to talk to this person. Here was someone who saw the value of having a will. Might he have been able to recommend a good Will Writer to his friends? A Will Writer that he had built a good relationship with. Sadly we will never know. But I can tell you that the Will Writer is no longer in the will writing business. Could the two things be connected? I wonder!

# It helps to be specific!

Very few business owners, let alone marketers, truly understand marketing – well good marketing that is – and I must confess that I didn't either for many years. And, even today, I still have a lot to learn on the subject.

The problem is that most business owners think that they can say anything, to anyone, anywhere, and they will get some business. And of course a few do. So, they just do more of the same and, with luck, they get some more business. Now I expect you've heard someone say, "I tried that, but it didn't work." You may have even said it yourself. But, have you ever considered why it didn't work, or have you just blamed the media used?

A few years ago I was asked if I could help a personal trainer, maybe mentor her as things were not going too well with her business. So, I arranged to meet her for coffee, to see if I could help her, and to see if we could work together. It turned out that she had been in business for about eight months, sort of had two clients, but had totally run out of money. Many new business owners massively underestimate how much cash it takes to start a business, but in this case she had started off with a fair amount. So, that wasn't the reason. In fact, she had a good amount more than she needed. So, I asked what she had spent the money on. Another common mistake, made by new business owners, is to spend their investment cash on the wrong things. Most often, a nice new car. But, no, once again, she had spent her money on the right things: marketing and advertising. However, this is where everything had gone wrong.

As a new business one thing that you can be sure of, is that as soon as your phone number becomes public, every single person in the world will be calling you to sell you whatever it is they sell. And, of course, one of the worst of these, is anyone selling advertising, because, "..obviously you need customers…" they say. And, of course, you do need customers, so you say, "Yes please!" But then another advertiser calls, and then another, and another, and another. And, very soon, if you are not careful, you have run out of money. But, it's not a problem, because they all promised you loads of business, and your phone will start ringing very soon. And you will make lots of money. But it never works that way. The personal trainer had spent money with eight different advertisers. I had a good idea that none of them would have worked as she told me about them, and, sure enough, she hadn't had a single enquiry. If only she had spoken to me first, I could have saved her a fortune.

So, why hadn't her advertising worked? To answer that question fully I would almost need a whole book on its own, so I will just cover a few of the main reasons here.

Firstly, she was media led. People just rang up, good sales people, whose job it was to sell her advertising space (most don't care what is in the space) and that's what they did. Media should have been the last thing she considered. Let me explain why. Top of the list is, does the media, whatever it is (door drop, newspaper, directory, online directory, calendar, diary, sports ground banner, magazine, TV) reach your target market? If not, forget it. Because nothing else matters. If it does, you then need to consider other things. Top of the list here is distribution. Again, if it's not distributed where you operate, forget it.

I once had a client call me extremely excitedly because he had done this amazing deal with a publication for some space. Until, that is, I pointed out that the magazine wasn't delivered in the area he worked. Still, it saved him a fair amount of money.

So, the thing about marketing is, is that first you need to know who your target customers are. Then you need decide what you are going to say to them. And only then do you think about the media. Where do your customers hang out? So, always think, Market, Message, Media.

Her other big mistake, well two mistakes, were that she had no idea who she was advertising to (her market), and so she had no idea what to say to them (her message). Her business failed, not because she was a bad personal trainer, but because the right people didn't know she existed.

Many people use this scatter-gun approach to advertising (marketing and selling), either because they don't know any better, or else, because they are trying to reach everyone, frightened that they will miss out on a sale if they market to just one type of client.

Don't believe me? Well think about Virgin Airlines. They don't advertise to everyone at the same time. They have separate adverts, for First Class, Business Class and Tourist Class (and others). All have different words, pictures and themes. But, everyone travels on the same plane.

Think about water. Everyone drinks water. But, how many different ways is it advertised? I've just Googled water. It's amazing – prices from 24p to $219 per bottle. Very different advertising and I bet Fillico Jewelry Water isn't advertised to people that are thirsty!

It's hard to convince business owners that they are missing out on sales because they are advertising to everyone and that they would make more sales if instead their marketing was targeted. No more was this the case than at a referral skills workshop I attended.

The trainer was doing her best to convince an attendee that it was the case. The person was a caterer and said that they could supply food to anyone. The trainer asked who were their ideal customers. Eventually the caterer decided on 'Ladies who Lunch'. Much better, but how about naming an actual lady? This was almost too much for the caterer, but in the end they said 'Jerry Hall'. The trainer turned and asked the other attendees, "Does anyone know Jerry Hall?" Silence. Then a hand went up. And this man said, "I don't know Jerry Hall but I do know the person who baby-sits her Bunny Rabbit. Is that any good?"

The thing is that ladies who lunch have money, and ladies who have Bunny Rabbit-sitters also have money. The caterer didn't get to meet with Jerry Hall but they did get two other ladies that lunched (and who had Bunny Rabbits).

Now this might be an extreme example but until the caterer had really targeted exactly who they wanted to speak to they hadn't recieved any referral interest, but by really targeting a market, they picked up two new clients. So, why does this work? Well, just think about it for a moment. Do you know any ladies who lunch? I'm guessing not (not off the top of your head anyway). But, how about, do you know Jerry Hall? The answer to that can only be, yes or no. And it's the same with your advertising. If it's not targeted at your ideal client, they don't know it's for them. But, if the marketing is targeted, they either know it is, or it isn't.

So, remember, you don't have to be terrific but it helps to be specific (I heard that somewhere and really like it). Work out your target client, then what you want to say to them, and, finally, where you will find those people. Get it right and you really could reap the rewards.

# A common interest!

Sometimes you come across a person whom you just don't get on with. Don't know why, it just happens. Once, when I was a BNI Director, I had this member who saw me as the BNI police; some members see their directors that way. It's a pity. Well, this member was too 'big' for the little things that it takes to run a successful group and he became something of a 'challenge' to me.

Things got silly. And we had a bit of a 'battle' over him wearing his name badge. He wouldn't! I even made him a nice new one and posted it to him. Still no luck.

Then one meeting he was wearing his badge. I didn't say anything and played it cool. I wondered why he had chosen to wear the badge now. Maybe it had only just turned up in the post. I never did find out.

Over the months I had avoided speaking to him; even went out of my way to avoid him all together. Well, on my next visit, a funny thing happened. We met at the coffee pot and he poured me a coffee. He was wearing his badge. I said "Thank you", and we moved on.

Then something very unusual happened at the group. I should really say, at the, chapter because that's what BNI call their groups. A chapter is run by a Leadership Team of three people: the Chapter Director, the Membership Co-ordinator, and the Secretary/Treasurer. One afternoon, I received a phone call from the then Chapter Director. He told me that the whole team was resigning with immediate effect. I hadn't seen that coming. But, what was more, they were all leaving BNI. I'm not going to go into why they were leaving as it has nothing to do with this story, only to say that it had nothing to do with BNI.

However, it did give me a problem. I needed a new Leadership Team – and fast. A Leadership Team can make or break a chapter, so it's not just a case of picking three willing members. You also need three people that will, and can, work together. And, in this case, a team that were strong enough to recover from, not only losing a whole Leadership Team, but three members as well.

I made my short list of possible candidates and started making my calls. My first choice of Chapter Director and Secretary/Treasurer both said yes. But no one on my list was prepared to take on the role of Membership Co-ordinator. I guess because out of the three roles it has the most work to do, and, you could argue, the biggest responsibility. So, at the next meeting I was still short of a Membership Co-ordinator. There was one person I could still ask and I did as soon as I arrived at the chapter. They too turned me down. I was in what you might call a 'jam'.

I looked across the room and there stood my nemesis; again he was wearing his badge. I knew he would make an ideal Membership Co-ordinator, but I also knew that it wasn't his 'thing'. But, needs must, and so I made my approach and explained the situation. Without a moment's hesitation he said that he would be happy to help. I wasn't really sure what to say. But I was warming to this guy.

I had my team and they were great.

It's funny how things happen, but at the next meeting I attended my new Membership Co-ordinator was doing the 10 Minute presentation.

He opened with, "You all think what I do is boring, so I'm not going to talk about that", and with that he left the room. 'Here we go', I couldn't help thinking. But he returned a few moments later, and I was hooked. He was carrying a leather motorbike racing suit and crash helmet. I looked at the knee-pads which were scuffed; this guy could ride a bike. I'm a big fan of Barry Sheene, love the racing, but I'm far too chicken to give it a try. This guy was a racer; and at that moment my impression of him totally changed. All because of a common interest. It turned out that he raced his bike all around Europe, and, later on, I was to use a photo of him racing his bike in my first book.

But back to his 10 Minute presentation. It was one of the best I've ever seen, as he used his racing to link and explain what he did in his work. Very clever.

A few years later we were to be part of the same Leadership Team; he again as the Membership Co-ordinator. But the great thing? We got to know each other and I was able to recommend him to a good friend of mine because he is very good at his job. And he gave me a birthday present, a football

Polo Shirt, which I still wear today.

Getting to know someone can make a big difference to the success of your networking, and this can often take months, as in this case. But the important thing to remember is that it may not be the obvious things that lead to that 'connection'. In this case it was our common interest in motorbike racing that was the final piece of the jigsaw, because although I had already known the guy for two years, nothing else had bought us together.

So, when you are talking to people, building those relationships, don't forget the personal stuff. Because it might just be that you both like Spanish cooking, for example, that makes the difference, and not the fact that you offer a brilliant service.

# He didn't call me!

It might surprise you to know that, considering that I've been networking for a great many years and run workshops on the subject, I am a very shy person. Believe it or not, I find it very hard to speak to strangers. And, when I do meet strangers, I end up doing a lot of listening; not a bad thing when getting to know someone.

Some people might even think of me as pretty anti-social and, I guess, they may have a point, as I've lived in the same house for thirty years now, and I don't know the names of my neighbours. In fact, I could easily go a month or more without even saying hello to them and even then it might just be a nod. During those years we have had a number of different families either side of us and only one did I really get to know, just a little.

However, it's the lady who lived the other side of us that I want to tell you about. I can't remember her name; not sure that I ever knew it.

One night we had an amazing storm. Rain thundered down and the wind howled all night. It felt like our house might be blown away, everything rattled, I feared that the windows might be sucked out, and the noise outside, well, I didn't like to think what might be happening. The next morning I checked our house for damage and, I am pleased to say, all was okay. But in the road was part of someone's roof – part of a flat roof. Now the only flat roof I knew of was on my neighbour's house, but it was at the back of her house – not the front. So I knocked on her door and suggested we check. Sure enough part of her roof was missing. It was astonishing. The roof had been ripped off, blown over her house and landed in the middle of the road without hitting a car or killing someone. I'm not talking just roofing felt here, as a great slab of plywood had gone as well.

Being a 'good neighbour' and, as she didn't really know what to do, I covered the gap with plastic sheeting and told her that I would get a builder I knew to contact her. The perfect referral for the new builder in my group, I thought.

I didn't see my neighbour for the next month but when we both arrived home at the same time one evening I asked her how her roof was. Her answer surprised me as she said it was just the same, still covered with the plastic I had put on for her. Obviously I asked why. This time her answer shocked me; the builder I recommended to her had never called!

Embarrassed, I apologised on the builder's behalf, and you can imagine what I did next. It's enough to say that the builder would ring her that day to make an appointment.

This time I made sure that I saw my neighbour a few days later. Had she heard from my builder I asked? Yes, she answered. Brilliant I thought. Then she added, but he never turned up for the appointment and she hadn't heard from him either. What's more, she had found another builder and they were doing the job the next day. I felt humiliated. But, I had learnt a very important lesson. I would never refer anyone again without knowing everything about them first.

A few months later I bumped into my neighbour again. The roof was fine. And as we chatted she happened to mention that she needed her fence looked at. So, I said, I know a good fencing company, to which she replied, "What like the last one? No thank you." My reputation for good recommendations was gone and because of that the fencing company would miss out (and I knew he was good).

Over the next several months two things happened. Most importantly, the builder left our group but the other was that my neighbour (with the roof) moved out and we got a new one.

This neighbour I got to know pretty quickly, I even know her name, and it wasn't long before the opportunity came up for me to recommend someone I knew to her. She was having a great deal of work done.

But, I had learnt my lesson (this was early in my referral career), and I would only recommend people I knew well, because they were my reputation. Also, I would keep control of my referrals. I would check that any referral I gave was followed up on. In total, seven members of my group did work in my new neighbour's house and she was very happy with them all and the work they did. So much so that at least two of the people did work in her next house. We have new neighbours again now – perhaps it's me!

So, what did I learn from this, and how will that help you?

Well, first, never recommend someone unless you know them well and are prepared to risk your reputation on them.

Second, keep control of your referral; don't assume that your referral will be followed up on. People forget, so check to see how it is going. And don't forget to speak to your contact to see how things are going.

But, there's much more to it than that, as I discovered. One bad job can ruin the chances of future referrals for the whole group. There's no telling how many referrals I may have got over time from my neighbour (I know I lost one) if the builder had done a good job. Even if he had just turned up for a meeting he had arranged. But I do know how much business I was able to give other members of my group because each in turn did a great job.

And, the best thing, pick good people, people you know well, and you don't really need to keep control of your referral. Why? Because they are good; they do their job.

One last thing; if you are given a referral. Please do a great job because it will benefit everyone in your referral group.

# One hot summer!

A One-2-One can be a very interesting and productive meeting, and then, at other times, a complete waste of time. More often than not, the average One-2-One falls somewhere between the two extremes. I remember having a One-2-One with a lady on one occasion and being the gentleman that I am, we talked about her first. We talked about everything she did and how I could help her, for a good long time, and then it was time to talk about me. At that point she just got up and left. I always refer to this as having had a 'One'.

A somewhat better One-2-One I remember was with a gardener. We had a great meeting in a local coffee shop and I really wanted to do my best to help him. I liked the guy and we got on well, and he told me all about a new (sit-on) mowing machine he had just brought. It seemed that what he needed now were large lawns to mow. So, who did I know who lived in a big house? We parted with a warm handshake, both promising the other that we would do our best to find some nice referrals.

As I slid into the driver's seat of my car I was trying to think of people I knew with huge houses and who must have a lawn. The inside of my car was doing a very good impression of an oven; I just had to get my air-conditioning fixed. So, without another thought I drove to my local garage. As luck would have it, they had time to look at my car right then, if I had time to wait. I did, and so I was asked to wait in reception. Lawns and big houses was all I could think of, but I was getting nowhere. I made a mental note: I needed more friends with really big houses.

This wasn't good. I really wanted to help this guy. In addition, I knew that he was very good at his work. There had to be something that I could do. I looked up and smiled at the receptionist and she smiled back. I went on with my thoughts. And then an idea hit me! With that I got up and crossed the room to the lady sitting behind the reception desk. "Hi", I said.

I then told her everything about my friend. All he did, about his new, sit-on, mowing machine, and how good he was at lawn-cutting. She seemed really interested. I then went for the 'kill'.

"Do you have a lawn that needs cutting?" I asked. "Sorry, but I don't have a lawn." She replied. Quick as a flash, I said, "Do you know anyone that does?" "No." She said.

"Oh", was all I could think of to say and returned to my seat. For a moment I just sat there. Then I started to think again. This had just been a set-back, I wasn't going to be beaten. After all, I was good at this sort of thing. I had my reputation to think about. It did occur to me that I didn't have to tell any of my friends about my failing. I was better than this. I never did figure out why I had such a 'bee in my bonnet' as my mum used to say that day, but I did. Maybe it was the heat. Anyway, off I went to reception again.

"Hello. We just spoke," I said. Not sure why I said this, as one, it had only been a few minutes since we spoke, but two,

I was the only other person in the room, and she had been watching me.

I reminded her that I had told her about my friend. He cut lawns. She nodded, remembering. I then went on to explain how we were both members of a local business networking group and, in fact, we met just up the road, over breakfast. I told her that there were lots of us. I think she was getting a little worried at this stage. At least she kept looking at the door to the workshop. I further explained that we were all in different businesses, we had a plumber, electrician, builder, accountant, printer, web designer, personal trainer, solicitor, IFA, SEO person, mortgage broker, dentist. I pretty much listed the whole chapter.

"Do you need any of those?" I asked.

"No," she replied.

"Oh." I said again and turned toward my seat. I just couldn't believe it.

"Excuse me," she said. I turned back and she continued. "But I do have two doors lying in my hallway. I don't suppose you know a good carpenter?" I could have jumped for joy.

"I know a very good one," I said, calmly, "I'll get him to call you".

With that the workshop door opened. My car was all fixed; it had just needed to be re-gassed. I paid my bill, thanked the receptionist, and left with a nice referral in my pocket.

Now, I'm not suggesting that this is a great way to get someone a referral. It's certainly not a way that I would teach anyone to find a referral. But, to a degree, it does prove a point.

Several years after this incident I met Nigel Botterill, of the Entrepreneur's Circle, and he has a maxim. 'If I had to do X by Y, or else I would die, could I get it done?' And, I guess, I proved that if I really had to find a referral I could. And this is a great question to ask yourself. Just think about something you need in your business and run the question. For example: if you had to get one new customer by next week, or you died, could you do it? I'm sure that the answer would be 'Yes'. So, why doesn't it happen? Because, sadly, it's not important enough to you. Use Mr. Botterill's maxim and, I think, you will be surprised at how much more stuff you will get done.

# Say it with flowers

Thank you can be a hard thing to say or at least, at times, it seems that way. And I learnt this as a young employer of staff, when my staff told me I didn't thank them enough. The trouble was, my staff were only doing what I paid them to do; nothing more. So, why would I thank them? How naive could I be?

I soon discovered that people enjoy life a great deal more when they are thanked. And, when people are happy, they work harder. But, more than that, they will do more for you; a great deal more. So, you would be silly not to thank people for doing their jobs, and really thanking them when they go 'above and beyond'.

Referrals are the major part of any serious networking group; in fact they are the only reason that some groups exist. At these groups there is a contribution part of the meeting where referrals are passed. When I was a member of one of these groups my goal was to give, on average, one referral every week. I think, I am right in saying, that in my ten years of membership I achieved around .97 of a referral (maybe I should have had two as my target). But, whereas, I found visitors relatively easily, referrals were for me always more difficult. But, I still got my one a week (well almost). So, at times, it was with horror, that I saw the way some members accepted the referrals they were given.

There was this one instance where, when it got to his turn, a member got up and walked across the room, saying he had a referral for another member. Because of the way the room was laid out the person had to approach the recipient from behind.

He held out the referral but there was no movement from the other member. In the end he just placed the referral slip on the table in front of the other member, got a grunt for his troubles, and returned to his place. It was just amazing. No thank you of any kind.

Now think about this for a moment. We have no idea how much effort the member had to put to find this referral, but more, how likely is the member to ever look for a referral for this ungrateful member again? Never?

Saying thank you for any referral you get is so very important. A smile and a hand shake should be the very least someone gets for their effort. Not only is it polite but it's also good business. But should it stop there?

How else could you thank those that give you referrals? And why stop there? What about staff? Customers? Suppliers?

How much better would they all work for you if they were thanked every once in a while? So, what can we do?

As I've already said, the least you can do when you are given a referral, is to give the person a hand shake and a big smile. But how about if that referral turns into business? And then repeat business? What if the referral is for a major piece of business?

How could you thank them then?

Well, there's the obvious, a quick note by email. Thanking them for the referral and letting them know that you have been in contact with the person they referred. This would not only show them that you valued what they had done for you but also that it meant enough to you that you acted on it straight away. These are both things that mean that person will most likely look for another referral for you.

But, how much better would it be if you phoned the person instead? You actually found the time to make a call and thank them for the referral again. If it was the case, you could let the person know that it was just the kind of referral you like. That could lead to more of the same kind of referral. You could ask them how they had come across it. If a lot of effort had been involved maybe a bigger 'thank you' would be in order.

Then of course you could send a 'Thank You' card. Don't know about you but when I get a lovely, hand-written card in the post, it's special. And I usually keep them. If you have taken the time to find a card, write it, and post it, it says a great deal about how you value any referral you have been given. It may only be a small thing to you, but to the person receiving the thank you – it's special.

You could always say 'thank you' with flowers; how lovely is that? Or, how about taking someone out to dinner or the theatre? The possibilities to say thank you are endless but the results will always be the same, happy people that know you value what you have done for them.

One of the best 'thank you' presents I ever received was a book. It was a book that I had wanted for a while. Now what did that say about the person who gave it to me? Well, certainly that they knew something about me, and had taken the trouble to buy the book. It was pretty clear that they were happy with my referral.

And there's something special about giving a gift: one you have thought about. The person who gave me the book, (it cost £9.35), could have just given me a ten pound note. More in strict money terms but what an insult that would have been. I would have given it back and thought the person a cheapskate. Odd how we think, isn't it?

One of the best 'thank you' presents I ever gave was to the wife of one of my staff; I did it just a few times. A bouquet of flowers sent directly to her (not via the husband). The reason was that he was doing an enormous amount of overtime and it really helped my company. But it meant that he wasn't home much. She was absolutely delighted with the flowers, and never made any fuss when he told her that he would be working late again.

Sadly I had to learn to say thank you. Don't you make the same mistake and I promise you will be rewarded.

# Just having a coffee

Truly successful networking is all about building great relationships; getting to really know someone. I expect that you have heard the saying, Know, Like, Trust. It's pretty simple. Before you will do your best long-term business with someone, you have to know them, like them, and trust them. Because at the end of the day we all like doing business with people we like and that is why I think 'like' is the most important of the three. After all, when you meet someone for the first time and you get to tell a friend about the person, you don't say I met this person and I really got to know them, or I really got to trust them. But what you do often say is that you really liked them.

And there is no better way of getting to know someone than having a cup of coffee with them. Having what is called a One2One. Obviously it doesn't have to be coffee, it could be a beer, a glass of wine, a pina colada, dinner, breakfast, the important thing is to meet and get to know the person and find out if you may be able to help each other in the future.

Now having a coffee with someone is fine up to a point because you will certainly get to know them and hopefully like them. But actually to be of real benefit to both parties, as with all things, you need a bit more of a plan. I've seen so many One2Ones end up being just exactly what they were, a cup of coffee with someone, and maybe a tick in a box, but in truth nothing much more.

Now I'm not going to insult you by telling you what you should take along to your meeting, but a pen and some paper would at least be a start. I promise you that you would be surprised at the number of people that turn up with nothing, I've even, on more than one occasion, had the person I was meeting turn up without any cash (or credit card) to buy a coffee. Trust me – not a great start.

So, you've got all of the basics with you, but what else might you take along with you? Now to a degree this will depend on how well you know someone. Is it your first meeting ever? Or is it maybe your eleventh?

Because that's another thing; a One2One is not just a one-off event – done that one, tick in the box, next please – it's about growing a relationship. I once met a lady who boasted about having twelve One2Ones in a week. What a waste of time. How could she possibly have helped any of the people she met? Just think about your best friend for a moment. They didn't become your best friend because you spoke to them once and then moved on to someone else. It took time to build, and more importantly takes time to keep, the friendship alive. I'm sure that we have all had a best friend that we have lost contact with. We stopped talking to or communicating with them as much, and before we knew it, sadly, they were no longer a best friend. Well it's just the same in business.

Okay, a slight detour there. Back to what you might take along with you to your meeting. Something I take along with me when I have really got to know someone is my client list – well part of it. I found this really useful because however well someone can describe their ideal client to you it's never as good as that person just scanning through your client list themselves. I've been able to make some great introductions for people because someone has picked out the perfect connection for them that I just wouldn't have considered.

With this in mind often your mobile phone is a great place to start because most of your best connections will be in your Contacts Folder.

Something I'm often asked is what should you talk about in a One2One? Again this depends on how well you already know the person, but the following are a great start. Remember you are getting to know the person, trust them and like them, so you need to cover just about everything; not just business. Of course you can start with your skills, what you are good at, and the things that you have accomplished. Interests, the things you enjoy doing and talking about, these can really help you connect with people, almost more than anything else. And let people know about your dreams and goals, both business and personal. You will be amazed at how many people will want to help you achieve your goals.

Another thing that I think is important is proof that you are as good as you say you are. What stories do you have that could back this up? Have you testimonials from happy customers that you can show people?

And don't forget to talk about your networks. And I'm not just talking about business here; include your social networks, the football team you play for, choir you sing with, school PTA that you sit on, everything where you mix with other people. You just never know where you might find the perfect connection for someone. And don't forget to mention your partner's networks; I've done rather well from those.

But there is something else that often happens after a One2One; you discover that you weren't asked the questions that you really wished you had been. So, as Baldrick would say, I came up with a 'cunning plan' to ensure this didn't happen. I made a list of the top ten questions that I would like to be asked and then I did my best to get them asked. After a while, as getting people to ask 'my questions' was somewhat harder than I had thought it would be, I would give the people I was having a One2One with my list of questions, and suggested that we worked through them, adding that they could do the same in the future. That way I made sure that we covered all of the stuff I thought important. But then I discovered that a good friend of mine had taken this idea even a stage further. She actually included the perfect answer to each question, and used her sheet as an example of how the idea worked. Not only improving the other person's One2Ones, but also ensuring that they had a record of, and gone over in detail, each of her questions. How clever was that! It made an amazing difference to the recommendations (referrals) given by both parties.

And one last thing about having a coffee, don't forget to make a date for the next time you will meet and to note down what you said you will do for each other in the meantime. I promise – it will make a big difference to the success of those cups of coffee.

# Global Networking

International Networking Week was set-up by Dr. Ivan Misner (Founder of BNI) in 2007 and runs for one week, starting the first Monday in February every year. The goal of International Networking week is to celebrate the key role that networking has in the development and success of business today. Events are run around the world with tens of thousands of business people from all networks taking part, including students, community organisations, government. In fact, all interested parties.

All types of events are held, with the focus being to bring all networkers together to network and to learn from key leaders in the business world.

One February I organised a riverboat trip on The Thames, with the help of Turk Launches, for one hundred and fifty local business people, from all of the local networking groups, to get together and network for the evening. It was a great success and lots of fun. There was a little education, lots of prizes (can't remember for what), great food, a few drinks, and everybody networked all evening. My plan had worked, no one sloped off early - the benefit of networking on a boat!

However, it's the event I went to in 2007 that I want to talk about. It was called The Big Breakfast. The idea was to hold the biggest breakfast ever in history; all over the UK business people would sit down for breakfast at 7.00am on the same day. Every BNI chapter was involved in different locations across the country. The idea was not for every group just to meet on the same day, but for as many of them as possible to sit down together in one room. So, I was one of seven hundred people that sat down in a sports hall in Harrow one morning in February for breakfast.

I have to say it was quite something. Have you ever tried serving seven hundred breakfasts, at the same time, in a sports hall? The noise in the hall was also something pretty special; seven hundred people all networking at the same time. I could barely hear myself think. There was even a Caterham 7 car parked in the hall.

The event was going to be run along the lines of a normal BNI meeting. Can you imagine seven hundred 60 Second presentations? No, nor can I! Instead there would be just one 60 Second from each chapter. We chose our lucky member by drawing the name out of a hat. Some chapters had chosen their best speaker, others had gone for their best member. This led to some interesting, and some not so interesting performances. The only one I remember was by Ashley Winston, of Palmdale Motors, as it was his Caterham. Why was it so memorable? Because when it was his turn he leapt into the driver's seat and fired the thing up. Gave it half-a-dozen blips on the throttle – what a great sound – and turned it off again. He nearly choked us all to death with the fumes; totally amazing! But, Ashley is the one person I remember, and we are still good friends today.

We also had a video broadcast from Dr. Ivan Misner, welcoming us to International Networking Week, and then covering what he considered to be good networking practice. Things like, asking about the other person first, how important it was not to force your business card on people, giving before receiving.

I think overall the event was a great success, however, I can't remember if I ever got any breakfast.

But, it's one other person that stood out for me, and the others on my table, and I have no idea who he is. We were nearing the end of the meeting and referrals were being passed, one table at a time. I seem to remember, the Chapter Director of each chapter, getting up and announcing to the whole room how many referrals were being passed in their chapter. Then the members would pass the actual referrals around the table to each other. This meant that only one table was really involved at any time and this led to some members becoming rather restless. It is remarkable how even adults can't sit still.

Our table was busy passing their referrals around, or talking, I can't remember which, when a man came running by, well he was certainly moving fast and didn't stop, and lobbed a pile of business cards onto the middle of our table. As one we all looked at the cards sliding across the table and then at the disappearing figure. A moment later we had all returned to what we had been doing before the interruption. Not one of us looked at the cards, and no one sneakily slipped a card into their pocket (I checked). Why? Because, we were all totally, amazed.

We had just listened and watched Dr. Ivan Misner, the Founder of BNI and acknowledged networking expert, tell us all not to force our business card on anyone, and someone threw their business cards at us. It really was bizarre.

I really can't understand what this person thought they would achieve. It was wrong on so many levels; from just plain rude, to proving that he didn't listen, that he wasn't interested in learning, and there was only one person he was interested in – himself.

Thrusting your business card into someone's face is not a great way to start a meaningful relationship, so I highly recommend you don't do it. Personally, I've never kept the card of someone who has done it to me. Why? Because I know the person is only interested in themselves and not in me, their would-be client. Now you might be thinking that the only person who counts is you, not your client, and to some degree you would be right. But there is a right way and a wrong way of doing things, and long-term, demonstrating that you are non-thinking, isn't the right way.

# Are you leaving people in the dark?

Over the past ten years I've collected a great many business cards. It's almost impossible not to collect pockets-full of the things if you do any amount of regular networking. And it wouldn't surprise me, if you are anything like me, that you have piles of cards on your desk, and an even bigger collection in one of your desk drawers. One day, you promise yourself, you will do something with them all; like put them on a database.

It also wouldn't surprise me if, every so often, you have looked at those piles of cards and just swept them off your desk into the rubbish bin. Most of us have done it at some time. After all, if a card has been sitting on your desk for a year, or more, what use is the contact now? The answer: in most cases absolutely none at all.

But that's just one problem of collecting cards at a networking event. Here I want to tell you about another. It's a problem that I have a real thing about, so let me explain and, to help me, I conducted a little experiment to prove my point.

In order to do this, I went to a networking event that I had never been to before – and, as usual, I collected a pocket-full of business cards. I will admit that I went out of my way to collect as many cards as I could, but I assure you that on this occasion it was okay because my problem is not with the people per se, but with their business cards.

The following day, I sorted through the cards and made some notes and I think you might be interested in my thinking and how it might affect the business cards you take networking in the future.

In total, I had the business cards of thirteen people (well four-teen really as I spoke to two people from the same company) plus an instant email (they sent it to me as we were talking) as the person had run out of cards.

One card was thrust into my face, and the person didn't ask for my card in return, so it's gone in the bin! I then have half-a-dozen cards of people that I met who were very interesting and whose cards are all well-designed and printed and tell me what they do. All of possible use in the future.

I then have a card of a guy who was some sort of designer. I never really found out of what, as he talked in riddles. So, to be honest, not of much use.

Then there is a slightly oversized card, by about 2mm (so just a pain), from a high-end video production company (well that's what the card says), but in truth I've never seen such a poorly laid-out card in my life. Video is all about the visual image, and so must the business card be, for the best chance of success. Another for the bin, I'm afraid.

Next I have a stylish, chunky card from a lady who does wardrobe management. Perfect. Just three to go.

The worst! One of those odd-sized, cheap cards you can get on the internet. But, to make matters even worse, the telephone number had been scribbled out and PTO written below in rough letters. On the back, in actual fact, was an email address. Guess what they did? Wealth Creation – I don't think so!

Now a card the same colour (bright red) as my own. A nice clean card which says what they do. And they wanted me to contact them.

And last, but by no means least, a card from a web designer, a great guy, who's different. He opened our conversation by saying he is a 'story teller' and it even says so on his card.

So, my question to you, what impression does your card give after the event? Have you ever stopped to wonder what happens to your card? Is it, and more importantly, are you remembered, or does your card just end up in the rubbish bin?

Is your business card worth keeping?

I ask this because all too often I am handed a card that just has a name and a mobile phone number on it. Sometimes it will have a company name, but often the name gives me no clue as to what the person does and the email address is no better.

If your card is anything like this, the chances are that it will end up in the rubbish bin. After all, I can hardly ring you up and say, "I've no idea what you do, or where you are based, but let's do some business." It's just not going to happen!

Now you might be thinking I'm not very good at networking, as having met someone I can write notes on their card (not possible with some cards), which of course I do. But, and it's a big but, why take the chance on someone else making notes about you, when you have the perfect opportunity to tell them exactly what you want them to know? Why risk your business card ending up in a bin somewhere? Wasting the very valuable time you spend networking, let alone the cost of the design and printing of your cards.

In any market place you need an edge over your competition: that something extra. So, why not increase the odds of your business card being kept, improving the chance of future business, by simply improving the information on your business card? That way your card might even make it on to that database.

# All to save £1!

In referral groups in order to get great referrals from your fellow members you must get to Know, Like and Trust them. In other words build a relationship with them and the stronger and better that relationship is the more referrals you will receive. In most cases. There are always exceptions.

Some years ago I was a member of a BNI chapter, as a printer, and was given a referral by a member for some business cards. Let me set the scene for you.

I had been one of the founder members of the group, there from the very beginning, when three of us had met huddled around a gas fire in a draughty club house on a golf course near Heathrow. Well this was about four years later and the person who gave me the referral, at the time, had been a member for about a year. In that time we had got on pretty well I thought and we had had a couple of One-2-One meetings. Our relationship was building well.

The printer in most referral groups gets a fair number of referrals. Let's face it, every business needs printing, and it's easy to think of something that you need a quote for when push comes to shove. Bit cynical you may think, but having been a printer in a referral group for ten years I can assure you it does happen. But I was never really bothered because it didn't happen too often and I did very well overall. But that's not the point of this story.

So, back to that referral for business cards.

It was a simple referral. A quote for 250 digital business cards, full colour, on one side of a 350gsm board. I emailed my price, £39.00 + VAT, over that morning, offering a delivery date and asking if they would like a sample of the card that I would be using.

At the meeting the following week along with the member business card box came a second small box. On the box was the name of a printer and in the box was a set of new business cards. The cards were for the person I had received the referral from the previous week. I have to say that I was more than a little surprised.

After the meeting I asked the member if they would tell me why I had lost the business and he said because he had managed to buy them for £38.00 + VAT. My quote was just £1 more. I didn't know what to say, so I just replied "Oh", and then added something about buying at the best price then.

Now you could read all sorts of reasons into why this happened. For example, our relationship wasn't quite where I thought it was, to that the member was actually very short of money. But I don't think it was anything more than just buying on price. That and not thinking.

Not thinking is something that I believe a great many members are guilty of in referral groups. You see, the point is that you have to build trust, get to know the people, get to like them and that requires thought. So, let's look at our £39.00 business cards. Where could things have been improved?

Well, first I could have followed up on my quote quicker. Who knows what the outcome might have been then? Obviously the member could have rung me and asked if I wanted to match the better price. This not only would have told me about his buying habits and allowed me to take that in to account with future quotes, but also it would have given me a wonderful opportunity to impress him. But let's look at what did happen.

The first I knew he had new cards was when they were passed around the table at our meeting. How do you think I felt? How would you feel? At that moment, do you think 'goodwill' was being built? You might be thinking it was only £39.00, 'get over it', but the point is it went much deeper than the money. What did it say about our relationship?

Then of course the cards were passed around in another printer's box. Every member saw that, plus of course the visitors. What did that say about me? 'We have a printer in our group but I use someone else'. It's not exactly a great recommendation and anyone who didn't know me would hesitate before using me. Was it because of price? Was it because of quality? Was it something else?

And then of course there is the missed opportunity of getting to know me better and finding out more about my business. Would it be worth spending £1 to find out more about me and my business? I certainly think so. Would it improve the chance of receiving referrals from me?

When I refer someone I am making a recommendation; I am putting my reputation on the line. So I want to know everything I can about the company and I certainly want them to be one of my suppliers if at all possible. How better can it be that when you are recommending someone and you are asked "How good are there?" That you can answer, with certain knowledge, that the company is great, and even better to be able to add, "…and they handle all of my business"?

Because unless you can say that, if you are using someone else, what does that say about you, and your recommendation?

Forget me for the moment and instead imagine that you are recommending an IFA. You assure your contact that the IFA is brilliant and that they will make them lots of money. And then they ask you the question, "What have they done for your investments?" And you answer, "Oh, they aren't my IFA." So you are recommending to your contact an IFA that you don't use yourself. What exactly does that say? How do you explain it?

So, my recommendation is, that even if it costs you a few pounds, use the people that you are hoping to get referrals from. Find out about them and start to build that goodwill. Because long term few great referrals come from people that you don't have a very good relationship with.

# No competition

There are many types of networking group and they cover almost every level of networking you could imagine and every time of day. From the 'one-off' events to those that meet weekly around the world. You can pretty much network every hour of the day, seven days of the week.

For example; Business Biscotti, who hold free events where anyone can drop in for a coffee and network, to 4 Networking who hold fortnightly meetings for their members, again anyone can join and attend whenever they want, to BNI who meet weekly, but who limit membership to only one person from each business category and membership is by an application process.

These different levels of membership make it possible for everyone to network, with many people being a member of more than one organisation, not only to suit their needs and availability but also their temperament. Some people just can't get up early. Others can't commit to weekly attendance. While others just don't like rules and regulations. The great thing is that there is networking to suit all types and tastes. Of course the results vary immensely, and these tend to mirror the level of commitment to the group.

One of the great selling points of BNI is that membership is limited to only one person from each business category. And I have to say that this 'No Competition' for business (referrals) within the group is a major factor in BNI's success, since it was founded in 1985 by Dr Ivan Misner. Whereas I can clearly remember being at another networking event where

I was the fifth printer to speak; as far as I know none of us joined the group.

However, what I have learned is that this 'No Competition' feature of groups like BNI is only partly true, because competition doesn't just come from your direct competitors. And this fact is true of all networking groups whatever their make-up. Let me explain why.

I'll use BNI as my example because the challenge is only worse in non-restricted groups, because of those direct competitors.

The average BNI chapter has around thirty members, which is great for business, but does increase competition. You see the thirty members have to each remember what sort of business the other thirty members are looking for. The problem is they don't. And it's something I have proven on a number of occasions. So, what can we do about it? What can you do about it?

My research shows that some members retain as little as 30% of what is asked for in a 60 Second pitch; with the best members remembering around 80%. Now this can be down to many different things: like being given something worthwhile to remember in the first place and not being given anything to remember at all. One of the best ways to remember things is to take notes, as not only do you then have a written reminder, but with some people the simple fact of writing something down helps them to remember whatever it is. BNI have developed the 'Referral to Look For' sheet which is given to members, in most chapters, to enable them to take notes. But having notes is one thing, using them is another.

So, what is to be done? If you're lucky 50%, of your fellow members will remember what you say, and most of the members may take notes, but how do you know they will be put to use?

Well, the first thing you need to do is make sure that you are one of the 40% of members that most of your fellow members will remember. I say 40% rather than 50% because there will always be some 60 Seconds that different people remember due to friendships and common interests. Don't forget this is competition for being remembered at this stage – nothing more.

How do you do it? By being interesting, different and clear. By standing out from everyone else and providing simple instructions of how they can help you. By doing the hard work, so they don't have to. Say the same old wishy-washy thing every meeting and guess what? You'll get the same old dull results. In this case, very few good referrals, if any at all. You need to ban words like: anyone, anywhere, everyone, and phases like: all the people you know, all business owners, from what you say.

Now this will mean preparation. So never go to a meeting without having prepared first. It's amazing how many people just stand up and 'wingit' and expect to get great results. Do they really think that any professional speaker gets up to speak without having done hours of preparation? Of course not! And then you have the members who either can't be bothered to fill their 60 Seconds, or can't think of anything to say. And again are surprised that they don't get many referrals. Can you imagine Virgin (Richard Branson) not putting any effort in to one of their adverts, or doing the same old boring thing time after time?

Okay, so you have now created a brilliant 60 Second pitch (you need another one next week) but there's still something else that you must do. Give the members a reason to act on it. Why should they put themselves out for you? Do they like you? Have you done something for them? Have you made it easy for them to find you a referral or to recommend you?

If you can put together a compelling sales pitch and give your fellow members a good reason to act on it, you really will be putting yourself head and shoulders above your competition, whatever kind of competition it is.

# Silence can be golden

Whilst eating all of those breakfasts I've heard many sales pitches. Be they 40 Seconds, 60 Seconds, or in fact just a few seconds, the quality of presentation and content have varied wildly from, at times, very poor to the exceptional. I have many examples of all types but for now I just want to tell you about one I heard many years ago and still talk about today.

It happened one morning in a group of which I was a member and at the time in charge of running the 60 Second part of the meeting. I always chose the order of the speakers at random because it means that every member of the group has to listen and is therefore far more effective. You have to be a bit more organised, but it is far better than just going around the room in order as, in a group of thirty members, you know if you are at the end of the line you have over thirty minutes until it's your turn. Therefore, there's plenty of time in which to switch off and get distracted.

I was about half-way through the group when I asked the next person I'd chosen to give us their 60 Seconds. This guy was big and confident, had a strong voice, and tended to fill the room with his personality so it was something of a surprise when he stood up and seemed lost for words. He just leaned his hands on the table in front of him and looked skyward. A few seconds passed and I thought that he was composing himself. After a few seconds more I looked at the rest of my team and mouthed "What shall I do?" No help there!

I glanced at my watch; twelve seconds had passed. Some of the members were becoming restless. Had he just forgotten what he was going to say? Was he okay? I looked again toward my team; still no help. I had passed the point where I thought I could say something, so I just sat and waited. Thirty seconds passed and he was still just looking at the ceiling. At thirty-three seconds he spoke, "It's very quiet in here. Just listen." And again, he just stood and listened to nothing. There were a couple of wise-cracks from the members. I thought 'too right'.

Then he spoke again. "Do you know why? It's because this room is double glazed. Look." And he pointed at the double-glazed windows. And then he said, "So if you know someone with a noise problem, you know where to send them." He finished with his company name and address and sat down to rapturous applause.

The brilliant thing about his 60 Seconds was not what he said or what he didn't say, it is the fact that he became a story worth telling. I recounted the story to a friend of mine a couple of weeks later, I would never of thought of them as a prospect for windows, and they spent £4,500 with him. And as you can see from this, I am still telling the story almost five years on.

There's one other thing about this 60 Seconds. Because it was so good I know that Karl was a member of the group that day, but I honestly don't know who else was. I can think of a couple of people that must have been, but I couldn't tell you the slightest thing about what they said.

Karl could have spent his 60 Seconds telling the group about how good double-glazing was for cutting out sound - maybe he had in the past - in truth I know that, but that day he became a story worth telling, and it wasn't even really a story about double-glazing, but it has resulted in a lot of business for him.

Becoming the 'story' is an amazing way of promoting and selling yourself, your products, and your business and the best thing is that it doesn't have to be about any one of those things directly.

When I recount this story I'm not talking about double-glazing at all, I'm not even really talking about Karl, I'm just telling a story about something I saw. How good is that? Just imagine what could happen to your business if you could get people talking about you and, better even than that, those people were still talking about you in five years' time. Now that really would be worthwhile free marketing and PR.

So, what is there about you, or your products, or your business, that you can turn into a story? Can you convey your message in an interesting way? In a way that will get people talking about you to the people they meet.

A number of people copied Karl's idea over the going months but none really pulled it off. To my mind the reason was because they were just copying the silence but for no real reason. Plus of course we had already seen it done. One person came close, an electrician. He held a smoke alarm above his head and said nothing. I expect that you have guessed what he did say, "That's the noise a smoke detector makes with a flat battery and your house is on fire." What he was selling was mains-wired smoke alarms; obviously a whole lot safer. He made his point; even if it was just to go home and check the battery in your smoke alarm. But it wasn't a story. There was no story about a flat battery causing a house to burn down, nor had he become the story himself.

The skill, the hard work, is to dig deep into your story and how you present it. The electrician had just taken a new smoke alarm out of a box and held it up. Just imagine how much bigger an impact it would have been if the alarm had been blackened with smoke and he had told a real story of how a house was destroyed but luckily firemen had rescued a mother and two young children. Adding, would you risk that on a flat battery?

Completely different, and don't tell me that mains-powered smoked alarms haven't just gone through your mind. I promise, do the hard work, and you will see a big difference in your sales.

# 9870 minutes

The thing about eating 987 breakfasts is that it also means that I have seen 987 Ten Minute presentations. It also means that I have seen a very, and I mean very, varied level of performance in the delivery of those Ten Minutes.

Something that always comes up is the subject of using technology, especially when I am running a Presentation Skills workshop. I normally recommend not to use it, unless it is integral part of the member's business, as, more often than not, it goes wrong: from the very simple - no power socket, to the very electrifying - when a projector blows up. I've seen just about every possible thing that could go wrong, go wrong, when using technology. There was a time in my own group when all that was needed was an extension cable and, can you believe, out of our six tradesman not one had a lead in their van? In the end I popped home to get one. And then there was another time, the setup was perfect, everything worked. Only problem was the member's presentation was on a memory stick back in their office.

But, even if all of the technology works, we are then left with the PowerPoint presentation itself. And, I have to be honest, these can be pretty dire. But none so much as one I remember, given by a dentist.

Everyone faced the screen, well I guess they would, other than the member giving the presentation that is. They sat at a table with their laptop in front of them, facing us, between us and the screen. During the whole ten minutes the member didn't look at the screen once. Nor did they move from their chair, and only occasionally did they look up at their audience. However, what they did do was read every word on each slide verbatim. And a great deal slower than we could read it ourselves. It was almost surreal.

What made it worse was that the presentation wasn't even very interesting. Most of the slides were just full of small black text. It certainly didn't help the member to get any more business.

If I had my way, every person thinking of giving a PowerPoint presentation would have to read 'The Presentation Secrets of Steve Jobs' first. It's a brilliant book by Carmine Gallo and I can't recommend you getting a copy highly enough. It's just amazing!

The snag is that most PowerPoint presentations are boring and so have little effect on their audience. There are a number of reasons for this. And top of this list is too many words. The trouble is the typical PowerPoint template. On the page there will be a title, bullet point, subbullet and maybe even a sub-subbullet. This layout might even be repeated a number of times on the page. The result? A page full of text and, in most cases, not very interesting text.

Think of the slides you have seen. Aren't most ugly, with too much information, too many fonts, and no styling? Isn't the type usually too small to read and don't most have way too many bullet points?

Your PowerPoint presentation should complement what you are saying, not be what you are saying. There is a big difference. A PowerPoint presentation is a visual experience; not just you swapping words that you say for words that an audience can read. None of us go to the cinema to read lots of words; we go to watch pictures. So, your presentation should be filled with great images and some slides may have just one word on them.

In his book Gallo suggests avoiding the use of bullet points, focusing on just one theme per slide, using as few words as possible, using photographs and images, and creating a presentation that is visually aesthetic. Overall, create a story. So, what have I learnt about using technology? Two critical things I think; one, to only to use technology if it will add to your presentation, and two, write your presentation first and then work out how PowerPoint will support your presentation. Not the other way round; building your slides and then working out what to say.

As with all things, prepare very well. Try out all the exact equipment that you are going to use. If you are relying on someone bringing a piece of kit for you, do all you can to check that it will work before the big day. I've seen a whole presentation fall apart for the lack of the correct connector. Take an extension lead with you, as you just never know where the nearest power socket will be. Again I've witnessed major problems when a hotel has changed the normal conference room on the morning of the meeting. And check that your screen has somewhere to stand; some venues, believe it or not, don't have room for a screen.

Talking of venues, if your presentation requires the internet, and the venue has Wi-Fi, check that it works in the room you will be using. I've often seen an otherwise good presentation flop because at the key moment the web wasn't available because no one checked.

I've also seen, well not seen, a presentation because the file wasn't on the memory stick that the member had with him. The member was convinced the file was with him when he had left his office the previous evening. So have two copies on, of course, two different memory sticks.

And, lastly, have a paper back-up and hand-outs, just in case all goes wrong.

# We'll do it our way!

I expect that you have heard the failure rate for new businesses: twenty-five percent will fail in their first year, and almost half will have failed by year three. What you might not know is that forty-six percent of those failures will be down to incompetence. What surprises me is that more business owners, new or established, don't seek any help. I was twenty-one when I set up my first business and I couldn't get enough help. In fact I had two mentors, not that I knew that's what they were at the time, and I owe Graham Pearce and Peter Harris a great deal, as their advice and experience was invaluable to me.

But what I really don't get are people who won't take advice, when offered to them, from those that have experience; from people that have done whatever it is that they are now trying to do. For some reason they would rather ignore something that works and do something different. Now I'm not suggesting for a moment that we should just copy things, don't question them, and never do anything new. That's not what I mean. But what I do think is that if you know very little about what you are trying to do, and you can gain from the experience of someone successful (and that's key – successful) who does, then it might be an idea to follow their advice before you try doing something different.

The trouble is that most of the people that I've come across who want to do things 'their way' are usually motivated by their way of doing things involving less effort on their part.

This is not a great recipe for success.

Organising launch events for networking groups is a great example.

When I became a Regional Director of BNI one of my first jobs was to launch a new group (Chapter in BNI) in a new area. I received four days of intense training, got the advice of senior directors, a number of information packed manuals, all the tools I would need, and a top director to look after me – Charlie Lawson. What I had been taught was a system that worked and had been perfected over many years (the system has been used to launch thousands of chapters around the world).

First I had to get a group of local business people together. My target was twenty as that is when, BNI have discovered, a business group really starts to pay dividends. Then we would officially launch the group and invite along as many local business people as we could. This is part marketing for the group, part PR (Public Relations), part awareness for the local community, and part to gain more members and grow the group. A launch is a brilliant event and you can easily have over a hundred people attend.

Now there is a system, a system that works – if it is followed to the letter – which brings amazing results. A massive fifteen percent return. Send out eight hundred invites and one hundred and twenty people will attend the event. Guaranteed! As I say it's amazing. And, I bet, like I did when I was first told, you're thinking, 'Can't see that happening', or something similar. But, this was a system that was proved to work, so why change anything? The least that I could do was to give it the 'benefit of doubt' until I knew better.

I'm not going to give you all of the details here, but it involves twenty people sending out forty invites each to their contacts. It's all about working as a team. There is a standard invite letter, nice white envelopes are used, and addresses (with contact names) are hand-written, stamped with a First Class stamp, and the invites are followed up with two phone calls (by different people).

It's pretty straightforward but boy does it cause problems. I've seen C5 Window envelopes used because it's easier, even though the advantages of using good quality envelopes and hand writing them has been explained. I've seen horrible manila envelopes used because they are cheaper; for forty envelopes! I've seen people miss out parts in the letter because it took time to put them in. I've seen envelopes franked; because it saved licking the stamps. And I know people that didn't make the phone calls. And in every case the groups concerned didn't get the expected number of visitors.

I'll always remember my first launch for three reasons. Firstly, because it was my first, so no surprises there. Secondly, because I was absolutely shocked by what one member of the group did. This guy was with me all of the way, really positive, did all of his invites early, and helped coax the 'slower' members of the group. And then it got to invite telephone swap list week. As I said the idea is to make two phone calls to follow up on the invites by two different people. One of the reasons for this is that if someone has said to two different people that they will be coming to an event there is more chance of them actually turning up. It's just one of the little things that helps guarantee the fifteen percent success rate.

Well I had forgotten to mention the swap of lists (well it was my first time) until the morning that we were due to swap the lists. A little later in the meeting my 'star' member got up and said he was leaving the group – and was gone. I just couldn't believe it. It wasn't until a few days later that I found out the reason. He had made up his forty names and knew he would be found out when the list swap was made. Truly astonishing.

The third reason was the proof that the system worked. After the second phone call you rank people as to their likelihood of attending. This ranking I then gave to Charlie Lawson and he told me how many visitors we could expect. On the day of the meeting, ten minutes before the due start time we had just fifteen people in the hall. Charlie told me not to worry. When we started the meeting just those ten short minutes later the room was full; Charlie was one visitor short! I've never changed the system since, although some of my groups have, and every time the system is followed it works and every time it's not, it doesn't. And yet groups still do it their way. As I say, I just don't get it.

They was even a group that employed a company to make their phone calls – and just one telephone call at that. It didn't work. Why? Well, for one thing, it was just one call instead of two, but another reason was that the call wasn't personal. After all the telephone sales company's member of staff could hardly say that they were looking forward to meeting them on the day. That personal touch was just another of those little things that helps to get the fifteen percent success rate.

So, my advice to you, if you are new to something, ask for help and follow the guidance given, unless there is a good reason not to, but that good reason not to, doesn't include because it's too much effort.

# Caught in the spotlight!

Every year there is a European BNI Directors Conference and in the April of 2012 it was in Glasgow at the Glasgow Hilton, and I would be presenting in front of around 150 of my peers. Well, actually that isn't exactly true, as in the room there would also be Executive Directors and National Directors, who looked after whole countries, whereas I just looked after a small part of a county in England.

My big day didn't go precisely as I had hoped or planned and my performance resembled that of the proverbial rabbit caught in the headlights!

It had all started when our Area Director team (I was a BNI Area Director at the time) was asked to present at the conference. As a team we would all give our view (independently) on what we thought it took to be an effective leader. Then, as a whole, the presentations would come together to become something pretty special. Our presentation would become much larger than the sum of its parts. But then it all went wrong (for me), and I learnt a big lesson; not only about preparation but also about being professional.

I can't remember precisely when, but shortly before the conference, the focus of our presentation was changed. I can remember that it was after my PowerPoint had been submitted and the content had gone off to the printer to be included in the conference manual. So, now we had to adapt; but not a major problem.

I was standing at the back of the hall, lapel microphone in place and switched on, prompt cards in my pocket, Power-Point already loaded (and working), and the speaker before me was making their closing remarks. Our team was doing well.

As I walked toward the stage, someone said "Just do your best." Just do my best; what was that supposed to mean? Did they think I wouldn't do anything but my best? Were they in fact saying that my best wasn't good enough? With that thought in mind I stepped onto the stage and looked at my audience. But I couldn't see a thing. A spotlight was dead in my face and its light sparkled on the lenses of my glasses. I really didn't like that. Okay, just talk, I thought. "Hello, Glasgow," I said. And glanced at my first prompt card, only to find that I couldn't really see it; the spotlight was too bright.

Still no problem, I've got my PowerPoint slides to go by. Just one snag, the screen is behind me which would mean turning round (not a great idea) and, in any case, the slides are just there to add to what I'm saying; they didn't carry the content. One slide is just a picture of a BNI Lapel Pin. I've got a great story to tell about that but I can't see the prompt card to remind me what it is. I've told the story many times, so in truth I don't need the card, but for some reason on this occasion I really do need it. But I can't see to read it.

The other thing I've just realised is that I don't have any props, All of the rest of the team had used a Flipchart (or charts that they could refer to on the screen). It gave them something to do; had stuff written on the pages to help them. All I've got is an audience to look at and I can't see them. It's like being on radio. You can't see your audience, but that's not because you have a bloody great spotlight in your face. It's because the audience isn't there, and I wish this lot weren't. In fact, I wish I wasn't. The lights are not so bad if I look at my feet, but I can't do that. It's really bad to look at your feet. It's what I teach in the Presentation Skills workshop, but I can't remember why. The main thing is that it's not good, so I won't do it.

My slides are coming to an end. "Thank you for listening I say." And, I'm gone. As I reach the back of the room a technician asks me why I didn't speak up, couldn't I see them waving? No, I say. It seems the microphone was on full but they could barely hear me. Great!

I was reminded that I could only do my best. And that some players only get to play for England the once! Thank you! So, what went wrong? Apart from just about everything. Well, if I'm honest, I didn't really believe in the change of focus of the presentation. Not that there was anything wrong with the theme chosen, it was just that my part of it didn't really adapt from what I had done already. It was a bit of a square peg in a round hole.

But there was far more to it than that. And that was all down to a lack of preparation. At that point I had never been on a stage with a microphone; there should have been a sound check. Strangely up until that point, I had never been the sole person on stage and had a spotlight pointed at me. Then of course there were my prompt cards. They were just in my normal hand-writing using blue ink. If they had been written in black and bold, I wouldn't have had a problem.

And then there is the experience of being the only person on stage. No other person to work with, no chorus, and no props for me to literally lean on. Lots and lots of things learnt. The biggest of all was, if you are it, the only person on stage, no props, you really have to know your stuff and believe in it.

So, what can you learn from my embarrassment?

Firstly, to make sure that your PowerPoint slides are designed specifically for your presentation. It would have been inconvenient, and cost some money, to change mine, but then the slides would have been developed for the presentation I was giving. Obviously practise until you really know what you are going to deliver. Added to which, if a presentation is designed only for the actual theme chosen, it will have a much more natural flow. If at all possible practise on the actual stage (room) you will be presenting from. By doing this sound can be sorted out, and problems like spotlights will be highlighted. And, of course, by having a walk through, problems like I had with my prompt cards, would have been noticed, giving me time to go over them with a big fat black pen.

It all sounds so easy, and of course it is, in hindsight. But the lesson about when things go wrong, is that you learn from them, and then next time you do whatever it is, you don't make the same mistakes again.

Later in the day I overheard someone talking about my 'performance' that cheered me up. The lady concerned told the person she was with, "He's usually much better than that!"

# A great breakfast?

I wonder how many rashers of bacon I have eaten in ten years of eating breakfast at networking events? Sometimes there've been as many as five meetings in a week, with, I guess, the average number in the last few years, around three.

It's amazing what effect breakfast, especially the Full English Breakfast, can have on the normal businessman/woman.

Breakfasts can range from pretty much just a cup of coffee, to a smorgasbord of dishes, but it is the Full English that is most usual. And it is the breakfast, more than just about anything else, that causes the most aggravation at the average networking meeting. Over the years I've seen full scale battles over the type of sausage offered, the fruit made available, and even the lack of toast. I've witnessed a member leave a meeting due to fact that the venue had run out of food. To be fair to the venue concerned, the member was very late to the meeting.

But the worst thing I was ever party to was when a whole networking group was prepared to close down if they lost their breakfast. It was an absolutely crazy situation. The venue wanted to put their prices up, but the members didn't want to pay any more money. I know what you are thinking. Simple answer: move venue. But you would be wrong. The members didn't want to change venue. They liked the venue, they liked the breakfast, and they liked what they were paying. Several months later the group did move to a place where they could pay the same money, but for a better breakfast.

Now these members are missing the point of networking; well the dictionary definition of networking at any rate; because networking is about business and not about the size and quality of the breakfast. To my mind, even if the only thing on offer was a glass of water, even nothing at all, if I were doing business with the other members I really wouldn't care. Let's face it, you can pick up a breakfast just about anywhere, and at anytime of day (the all-day Full English).

That's not to say that a nice breakfast isn't a very welcome part of the meeting. But it's so not the most important thing. (Mind you, coffee on the other hand...)

However, I do think that venues, especially restaurants, are missing a trick with their breakfasts; training venues as well. I just can't understand why. Actually I can, it's because they just don't 'get' true marketing. In the main, recommendations; word-of-mouth. And, of course, personal choice.

So, what am I getting at?

The standard of breakfast of course! I've eaten all kinds of things for breakfast: Indian, fish, Japanese, pancakes, Polish, burgers, and of course the Full English. And I've eaten them in all sorts of places, from the smallest of restaurants to large hotels, and many of the big restaurant chains. And I have to say that, overall, the standard of food and coffee is poor. Quite often the service is poor as well.

Does this really matter? After all, it's only breakfast. And as I pointed out earlier, it's not about the breakfast, it's about the business. And that is my point, food is a restaurant's business. If the service is bad, and the quality of the food poor, are you going to go back to the restaurant for dinner? Will you recommend the restaurant to your friends? Of course not. You won't give the place another thought. But what a difference there would be if the service was great and the breakfast was cooked to perfection. Wouldn't you think about going back then? And wouldn't you go with a friend?

But the situation is even worse than that. I used to eat regularly at a well-known high-end restaurant chain, but not now, because their breakfasts were so often poor that I just stopped going there for dinner. And as for another well-known chain, their breakfasts were just as poor, so I avoid eating there as often as I can.

These restaurants have the opportunity to impress large numbers of local business owners every week and yet they do the opposite. Why? Saving money, on staff as well as food? Lack of thought? Or is that the general standard of their offering?

Whichever it is, they are missing out on thousands of pounds worth of potential business.

However, it doesn't stop there!

Providing great food and service is one thing. But what about actively looking for more business? There's so much restaurants could be doing on that front. Like coming to a meeting as a visitor. Can you believe that many venue owners don't even know what happens at a networking event?

Only once in my ten years of going to breakfast meetings has the venue done anything to tempt the members to come back. That is truly astonishing. And don't think that I haven't suggested the idea to a few good ones. But, as I said earlier, most restaurants just don't get marketing. After all, how simple would it be to give every person at the meeting a voucher for a glass of Prosecco for each of their party when they come back to dine? Maybe go even further and ask every member to join their VIP Diners' Club, now they know birthdays and marriage dates. It's just so simple.

Now, you might be thinking, what's that got to do with me? Well, the answer is very simple. Have you an opportunity to increase your sales, staring you in the face, but you are doing nothing about it?

# Full of good intentions

Workshops, training events, seminars, webinars, conferences. I bet, like me, you have been to a fair number. Because learning is one of the most important things that we do in life, and in business it's just the same. You must keep learning. And if you study the most successful people around the world, you will find that they are always learning; they never get to the point where they think they know it all.

And of course on top of all these training courses, there are also videos, books, audio CDs, and a whole lot more. There really is no excuse not to learn. In fact, have you a plan for what you will learn this year? Because you should have. How many workshops you will attend? How many business books you will read? How many CDs will you listen to?

Now go to any workshop today and you will see people taking copious amounts of notes, both written and typed into a computer. They may even record them, and even video the event. Pages and pages of notes; I've done it myself. And, of course, you often get course notes from the organiser. So, a vast amount of information.

The trouble is, learning is one thing, but unless you do something with the knowledge, it's not exactly a waste of time, but you aren't going to gain a great deal from it. The key is implementation, actually putting into practice what you have learnt. And this is where, more often than not, things go wrong, as back in the office, the notes are put aside because everyday life takes over again. And so nothing much changes. And, sometime in the future, another workshop is attended and the process is repeated again. And again, and again.

So, what can we do? Stop learning? Don't bother to take any notes? Well, no – of course not!

But, what you do have to do is follow through on those good intentions - the reason that you went to the workshop or read the book, in the first place. And here are a few ideas to help you, that I have found work for me, and that I suggest to those attending my workshops and events.

The first thing I do is highlight two or three things from each session of a workshop. So before you rush off for a coffee or the lunch break, (after all you will only stand in a queue, or worse, rush to your phone), spend a few minutes going over your notes and pick two or three key learnings. 'Star' them, put a big circle around them, or highlight.

The other thing I do, as soon as I am home, is précis my notes. At this stage I might even dump whole sections because either the notes I've made aren't relevant to me, or they just don't, the next day, make any sense (it happens). I also now underline things I think are important. By doing this I now have, not only clear notes, but also notes that are all appropriate to my needs. And at the very top of my text are my key two or three learnings.

There is also an added benefit to this 'tidying' of your notes. The re-reading and sorting will help you to better remember them. You will also find that as you go over your notes, without the pressure of listening to the presenter and trying not to miss something really major they say, you will question what you read and even imagine yourself doing what you read. This will further aid the process of remembering.

Another thing I do is to go over my notes again a week later and a month after that. I do this for two reasons; firstly it reinforces what I have learnt and so it helps me to retain more of it, and secondly, things I have forgotten, or I wasn't ready for at the time of the note taking, I may now be ready for.

So we have given ourselves the best chance of remembering what we have been taught. But, to make any real difference to our businesses, we still have to implement something. So, what now? Well this is where you need a plan and it starts with the three key things that you have highlighted. And it's pretty simple. When will you implement whatever it is? Any reason it can't be now? How will you implement whatever it is? Do you need money, expertise, extra staff? Or just the will to get started? And what result will you be looking for? How will you know if what you implemented was worthwhile?

For example, after reading this chapter and following my suggestions. Are your notes better and do you remember more?

Oh, one last thing about workshops and similar events. If like most people who attend these events you get fired-up by them, get full of good intentions, are more motivated after them, and even implement just a little of what you have learnt, that's great. And even if you are like the person who once told me, "It's great for 48 hours after the event but then I slip back to normal", you have the opportunity for major change. Now you might be thinking that there's little point in being more motivated for just 48 hours and then returning to normal, and of course you would be right. But how about this for a great idea? It's something that has worked for a number of my clients. Go to an event every month; plan your year of education and learning.

So, what would be the result if you did?

Well, one amazing outcome, would be that you were more motivated, than normal, for 24 days a year. That's pretty much a whole month. Just imagine what effect that could have on your business. Then if you only implemented just one item from each workshop into your business that would be twelve things you would have changed in a year for the better. And do you really think that if you were doing all of that it would be so easy to slip back to 'normal'? Somehow I don't think so! The thing is you would be breaking what is just a habit. But the best bit, it wouldn't take a year, because momentum would take over, as you would start to stay motivated for longer and implement more.

I've witnessed this with many of the people I mentor and I also noticed something else in my years of running workshops. The best business owners and the best networking groups both come to the most workshops. Coincidence? I don't think so.

# I'm an author

I've always enjoyed writing, but I've never been able to spell, even simple words, and my grammar is, well almost, non-existent. (Word has been very busy in just this one short sentence). It would also seem, according to my close friends, that I maybe a little Dyslexic – but I've never bothered to get myself tested.

At school I failed my English 'O' Level a number of times (both language & literature) but a wonderful, teacher, wouldn't give up on me, and eventually helped me to pass my exams (aged nineteen). I owe her a great deal.

After school I continued to write, but always in secret, and I now have a number of files full of stuff I've written. I have complete short stories, articles, pages of ideas, and fifty thousand words of a fiction crime book (I need another fifty thousand words to finish it).

As I say, up until recently, all of my writing was done in secret; just a hand-full of people knowing about it. But then I got to know someone, to like them, and more importantly trust them, and I told them about my writing. Now I had told a few people in the past that I wrote a bit, but none, up until this moment, had ever asked if they could read some of it. Not only was it a shock to be asked by this lovely lady but it also scared me. What if she thought my writing was rubbish and, worse, thought I was stupid?

As I say, by this stage, I trusted her and so showed her two of what, I thought, were my best pieces of writing. I watched her face as she read them, and I got the impression that she liked what she was reading. Having finished she said that she really like the writing but that the English needed some work. And I guess that is where my writing career really started.

Even then I still kept my writing pretty much a secret. Okay I trusted this lady, but she was very different to the world at large. However, amongst over things, I did get an article published in 'You & Your Baby' titled 'Home Birth – a man's view' about the birth of my third son. I seriously can recommend Home Birth, and I even got paid for my story.

My writing really started to improve and far more people got to know about it when, in 2008, I started a blog, called 'My BNI Day'. It started because of a chance remark by a soon-to-be Chapter Director. He wanted some help and to learn from my experiences in BNI. So I started to post, in secret, really just for him. I had two goals: one that what I wrote would be really useful to him and the other, that my blog wouldn't be a 'five minute wonder'. My second goal, I know I achieved, as I am still writing the blog today. The first goal only those that read it can judge. There is an interesting fact about the web, you can't keep a secret for long. Within a short period of time (my fourth post) Dr. Ivan Misner (the Founder of BNI) found my blog! Luckily he thought it was a good blog and agreed with what I had written. So much so, that he reprinted it in SuccessNet – the official BNI online magazine.

A few years later I was fortunate to be mentored by Ivan Misner, in his writing programme, having been recommended by BNI HQ (England), and a few years later this led to him writing the foreword for my first book, 'BNI: One Bite at a Time'. And it's that book that I want to talk about here. I know a number of people that want to write a book but for one reason or another they never get around to it. You might be just the same.

To start with, my big reason for not writing was that I didn't think I was good enough. If that's how you feel as well, all I can say is find someone you trust, and let them read your work. Another reason that stops people is that they don't know what to write about. The best I can suggest is to write about what you know about and are passionate about. Remember my first real story was about the birth of my third son.

Then of course you need to plan the book out. Again this is easier than you might think. You have your subject. Well what are the dozen or so major things that you want to say? These will be your chapters. Then when you have your chapters, what points do you want to make in each chapter? Three points for each chapter is ideal. Now you have the basic outline of your book. You could do the whole thing in thirty minutes.

Okay, now comes the hard part, actually doing the writing. My best advice here is just to start. Write anything – but just get started. What I find is that once I've started the words begin to flow, and it doesn't matter if I dump the first stuff I wrote. And that's a big thing; don't be scared of throwing stuff away. Just hit delete. If this really scares you have a document of deleted stuff. I still write a lot on paper and then dumping stuff is far easier. You just put a line though it, but it's always there if you change your mind.

Then of course you have to find the time to write those thirty, fifty, one hundred thousand words. Will you do as Ivan Misner did for his first few books and write late into the night. Or, be like me and write five hundred words a day. By writing just five hundred words a day you could have a fifty thousand word book completed in just one hundred days; that's just over three months.

But, the thing that stops most people from writing their book is in fact the writing. They start but they never finish. And this is where a good mentor comes in, and it doesn't have to be a professional mentor, but it needs to be someone that will keep you on track. Another idea for getting your book written is to give yourself a deadline and tell someone about it. With my BNI book I wanted to launch it at the BNI Directors European Conference so I had a date I couldn't miss.

Once you have finished your book I recommend the use of a good proof reader, as there's nothing worse than a book full of mistakes. Now something that I think is worth pointing out here is what I mean by a good proof reader. In my case I want someone who is going to check my spelling and grammar but who isn't going to try and change my writing style. Also an editor does a different job; they might want sections taken out, or added, or re-written. That can be tough!

So, you now have your manuscript. What next? How will you publish? You can look for a publisher, self-publish, print a real book or make it into an ebook. For myself I self-publish, print real books as I just love the feel of a real book, and then publish an ebook later on.

Whether you are going to print, or go electronic, I recommend that you get the help of a graphic designer to lay the book out. It just looks more professional. Then you need to find a printer; there are a number of good ones online. Something that you will need to decide on at this stage is how much you want to sell you book for and if you need an ISBN (International Standard Book Number). You will need to have an ISBN if you are hoping to sell through the major chains. I have my own ISBNs but most printers can supply you with them.

When printing, I highly recommend that you get a full printed proof of your book. It can save a whole lot of disappointment when you tear open the delivery box of your first ever book; I was a printer for over thirty years and have seen the 'look'.

Now of course the really big thing you have to do is sell your book. Without a plan, this can not only turn out to be expensive, but also soul-destroying. I printed thousands of copies of a book for someone once, and believe me I advised them not to do it, and they didn't sell a single copy. Not one!

So, what's the market for your book? Who will buy it? Where will you find these people? How will you get the book to your buyers? How can you get your book exposure? You might even need to think about where you will store your books. You really need to think about all of these things carefully before you place your print order. In truth, before you start writing.

With my first book, 'BNI: One Bite at a Time', I did two things that, firstly, took away any financial risk on my part and, secondly, got me a lot of exposure for my book. As I said earlier, I timed my book's launch date to coincide with a BNI conference, where I was given a few minutes to promote my book on stage to just about every BNI Director in Europe (around 250 people). The other thing I did was to have a pre-publication special offer. My offer was for batches of twenty or forty books at a very special price. This was a great success and, before I had even placed my print order, I had covered the books' total printing costs. Further, I sold every single copy of my printed book (including a small reprint) and it is now available as a Kindle. Something of interest here, is that on the Kindle, most of my sales are in America.

I hope that if you are a budding author that my story has given you the incentive to get started. Because if someone who is as bad at English as I am can write a book – then so can you.

# Have you booked your holidays?

When I first started in business there seemed to be two ways in which business owners paid themselves.

The first of these was based on taking as much money as you wanted out of the company and then paying the suppliers and (even staff) if there was anything left over. To my mind this system was totally outrageous and almost criminal. And I can remember many heated discussions on this practice. I was told that I was a fool and that everyone had a right to get paid – if they made a profit I thought and if that salary was reasonable. I was even told by one company director that at his age (he was in his late fifties at the time) he deserved a certain salary so that was what he took. Deserved? To my mind no one deserves anything; whatever it is has to be earned, however old you are. As a plan it was just stupid.

The second system, and the one that I back then adopted, was to take my salary from any profit, as a company, we made. Equally stupid, but at least it was moral. Furthermore, it was a system that seemed to work for me, my companies grew year on year, and my family (we have four sons) enjoyed our fair share of new cars and nice holidays. Two holidays that I really look forward to each year are skiing in the spring and sailing, off Corfu, in the autumn. As family holidays go, I don't think, you get much better.

But in fact both systems are wrong. But use the right system and you will see a major shift in just about everything you do.

The problem is that when you first start in business most of us just copy what other business owners are doing, and, in truth, without any real thought. It's not really the best of ideas for success, unless of course you copy someone who is very successful. Furthermore, especially in times gone past, your accountant or bank manager didn't help much; some are somewhat more enlightened today. Back then my bank manager was perfectly happy if I said I was going to sell ten percent more than the previous year, and my accountant just told me how much profit (or loss) I had made eighteen months previously. As I say, not a great deal of help. And of course a good mentor was hard to come by, even if you knew such a person existed.

Okay so what's a better way of doing things? Well, as with everything else, it's about thinking and planning.

Let's start with your salary. How much do you really want to earn? In fact, need to earn? There is obviously a big gap between what you really need to earn and what it would be nice to earn. But it's surprising how many business owners don't even know how much they need to earn a year in order to just survive. So, where do you start?

You start by thinking. First you write down all of your expenses for the year. Just normal budgeting. Then you think about all the other stuff that might happen during the year. Birthdays, Christmas, the odd weekend away, replacing that worn-out carpet in the hallway, decorating the spare room, the special anniversary that's coming up, your best friend's wedding, everything you can think of. That's what you need to earn. Then of course you can add: that special holiday, new car, moving house, the Gibson Custom Les Paul guitar you've always wanted (I have Pearl Export drums on my list – when I'm allowed to buy them!), again adding the things you would like. And that sum is what you want to earn.

Now you have a real figure that you can work with and it can go, along with all of your other costs, into your business plan. What you will find is that if you create an accurate plan for your business you may need to increase your sales by (for example) seventeen percent, which is far better than the ten percent you add every year just because it sounds like an okay number. Ten percent, 'it's a good increase'. Now you have a real reason to grow your business; because it will provide you with what you really need or want.

Of course you might find that having done your maths that you need to increase your sales by fifty percent, but I can assure you that knowing that is much better than not knowing; because you can do something about it.

The other thing this exercise might uncover is the need to do some hard work. But again, this is great, because you have your list of the things that you want as motivation. How much do you really want that new car? And how about this for an idea? In October book all of your holidays for the next year (Nigel Botterill does this). Not just think about them, dream about them, but actually book them. After all a holiday for the following October you won't have to pay for until the August. Now you might be thinking, 'Eh, wait a minute. This sounds like the take all the money you want, and don't worry about anyone else, system', but it's far from it. You see this is where the actual planning comes in, some serious thinking, and maybe even some hard work.

You have worked out how many more sales you need to do in the coming year over what you did in the last. From this figure you can work out how many more customers you will need to reach that target. Then, once you have the number of new customers needed, you can work out how you are going to get them. Now of course this could involve spending more money on marketing and sales, even on new staff (sales or production). If it does, these costs must be put back into your business plan, and the sums done again. You see, I said it was hard work. The great thing about this is that it takes all of the guess work out of what you are doing and, what's more, with a plan in place, you have far more chance of realising your chosen salary. Maybe of buying that new house!

Planning, or at least this level of planning, is done by very few business owners and if you become one of those that does plan in this detail you will be setting yourself apart from the norm and massively increasing your chances of success.

This lack of planning, and certainly the lack of real goals (big goals), became very clear to me in one of the monthly workshops I used to run. Part of this particular workshop covered what those present wanted to get out of their membership of the organisation (how much business). In the main the answers ranged from not really knowing to covering their membership cost (around one thousand pounds a year); very few people ever had a bigger target.

We would then discuss the time it would take, even to be an average member of the organisation, and what value this time might have. It's amazing how many business people don't put a value on their time; it truly amazes me. After all, time is one thing we can never replace. Eventually, I would get most people to come up with an amount; but even then, in most cases, it would be just a few thousand pounds. Next we would discuss their average order value; again very few people ever knew this. And, again, very few knew what there conversion rate was: how many leads turned into actual business.

You see without knowing these numbers you are definitely setting yourself up to fail. If you don't have a target amount of business you want, how can you judge if what you are doing is a success? Then if you don't know your average order value how can you possibly know how many orders you need to hit your target amount of business? And if you don't know your conversion rate, you have no idea how many leads you need to get those orders.

And obviously if you don't know how many leads you need you can't plan exactly what you have to do in order to stand any chance of getting them. You really are dead in the water! So, if you don't know your numbers, if you take nothing else from my book, please, please work them out. And if you really don't think you are up to it, your accountant (or bookkeeper) will be happy to help you if you ask.

To get you started: as a rough guide to know your average client value just divide your turnover by the number of (active) clients you have.

# It's bedtime!

There are 1440 minutes in a day, every day without exception, so no matter who we are we get exactly the same amount of time. Doesn't matter if you're Barack Obama, Sir Richard Branson, you or me, we all get exactly the same. But what is different, very different, is how we all use those minutes.

What I've found is that successful people value their time far more than ordinary people and are much better in how they prioritise its use. I've also discovered that they are prepared to sacrifice a great deal to achieve the best use of that time.

If you really value your time, it's easier to prioritise its use. And, if you don't actually have any more time, it comes down to what you are prepared to give up to better use that time. Even then, in both cases, you still have to use your time effectively for maximum benefit.

The problem is that most people don't realise that time is just escaping them and, of those that do appreciate the fact, most believe that there is nothing that they can do about it.

So, what do I mean, and what can you do about it?

Well, ask just about anyone, and they will tell you that there's never enough time to do everything they need to do. And they are certainly too busy doing 'real' work, to take time out to plan for the future of their business. The result? Nothing ever changes. Nothing is ever planned; so of course nothing can change. The problem is that they are too busy working, to give themselves the time to make any difference. It's the old Catch 22 situation. But does it have to be that way?

I started my first business as a 21 year old. I didn't have any customers, so I only had one really important thing to do each day. Find customers. So, every day I jumped into my car and went selling. No internet and Google in those days; the Yellow Pages at best. And I went all over the place. Then I ran out of money, I mean really ran out. Petrol was only .36p a gallon and I couldn't afford any! So, I was forced to target my sales activity to places that I could walk to. On my first trip, on foot, in my home town (Hampton), I made my first ever sale.

I couldn't believe it. I just hadn't been thinking. From that moment on my target sales area started on my doorstep and it worked rather well.

A tradesman client of mine used to spend the best part of everyday driving around to his various suppliers and jobs picking up and dropping materials because no one else was free to do it. I pointed out that it was a little like Sir Richard Branson driving the fuel truck around to his 747 Jumbo jets at Heathrow. My client now has a driver, who also does labouring jobs when required, and has the time to plan for the future of his business. To date, this has led to almost a doubling in size of the business. Again it was a case of not thinking and just doing what seemed obvious.

Then, of course, we have the people that are pretty time efficient, but who still want to do more. This is where you find out if something is truly important to you or not, because you have to make a sacrifice. You have to give up something else in order to find the time. And, usually, it's fun stuff that has to be given up.

But, sometimes, it's just sleep. Another client of mine was desperate to spend more time working on his business. But he just couldn't, or wouldn't, give up anything he was doing. I knew that he went networking one morning a week, so I asked him what he did the other four mornings. Answer? Got up later and watched some breakfast television. What I suggested was that he got up at the same time as he did for his networking meeting and started work (no breakfast TV). He gained eight hours a week.

One of the stories I like the best involves Dr. Ivan Misner, the founder of BNI, and how he went about writing his first book. Being very busy, and making good use of his time, and not wanting to disrupt his time with his family, he had to think of another way of making himself time. And, without the aid of a Time-Turner – Hermione had one in Harry Potter. So, twice a week for almost a year, at bedtime, instead of going to bed at 11.00pm, he did at least three or four hours writing. Ivan told me that when his first book was published he eldest son said to him, "You wrote a book?! When did you write a book?" Ivan wrote his next couple of books in exactly the same way. Now he tends to write all day every Wednesday and has done so for the past eight years. To date, he has now written 16 books.

If writing a book is something that you have always dreamed of, is it important enough to you to give up eight hours of sleep a week for a year to do so?

So, how else can you find more time?

Working smarter is key and I will give you a couple of ideas that you can use to great effect in a minute. But first, what about another sacrifice? Remember, giving something up doesn't have to be for life, it just needs to be until you have achieved whatever it is you want to do. Read the story of any Olympian and you will be amazed at the things they have had to give up, and you don't have to go anywhere near that far (well, in most cases) for success.

Another client of mine assured me that he had no time. But, I promise you, there is always time somewhere, it just depends how much you want it. During a mentoring session I asked him what he did with his evenings. And the answer was basically nothing. No, I didn't suggest that he could work all evening. But, I did discover that he watched television for an hour, a 'soap' that he hated, for no particular reason. It was just a habit. So, we broke the habit, and not only did he get the work done he wanted to, but he felt better for it.

Okay, a couple of ways to make better use of your time. Firstly, set end-times for everything that you do. We all set start-times, pretty hard not to, but few people set end times. In other words don't just let things take as long as they take. Set a time limit and stick to it. Also, set yourself deadlines. Not just on big things but on small things as well. And tell people about your deadline. It focuses the mind and also adds some accountability.

I often have one of my deadlines as a screen-saver on my PC.

Another major area where time can be saved is in meetings. Most people set a meeting time, an hour, two hours, half a day, all day, and then fill it with content. It is much better to decide on the content first and then work out the time needed to deliver it. Most people will appreciate a shorter, more concise, meeting than one that is padded out to fill the time allotted.

Time is arguably our most valuable commodity and certainly something we can't ever get back. But to get the best out of those 1440 minutes we have each day, it's not about cramming everything in that we can. It's about using the time wisely and deciding what we want to spend our time on. Including sleep at bedtime!

# Are you your assistant?

I first meet Nigel Botterill in 2010 and it wasn't long before I was 'introduced' to 'Botty's Rules' of business; the twenty nine success secrets from the UK entrepreneur who's been there and done it. His rules certainly made me think. And reading his book 'Botty's Rules' I have to say really changed the way I thought about a great many things in my business life.

I'm not going to re-count Nigel's rules here, but I do highly recommend that you get a copy of his book and find out what they are. I promise you they will make a big difference to the way you think.

Something that 83% of business owners say they would like more of is time. Personally I think the other 17% are not being entirely honest! But be that as it may, for most business owners there is never enough time to do everything you need to do – let alone the stuff you would like to do.

The trouble, especially if you work on your own, is that you have to do everything yourself. Or at least that's what you think.

It's an easy trap to fall into and we've all done it. There are a few invoices to type. Well we might as well do that. We need to pick up some stock and there's no one else who's going to do it. So we better had. And all those parcels that need to go to the Post Office? We can fit that in, in between meetings. Then of course you can build your own website and design your own business cards. It goes on and on. And then we come to our actual work.

Well it's certain that no one can do it as well as we can. There is just never enough time to get everything done.

Nigel has a saying, it's not a Botty Rule but it could be, that unless you have an assistant, you are an assistant. It's so true.

One of the first things I do when mentoring people is to find them more time. Why? Well for two main reasons. Firstly, because it reduces their stress levels and secondly, because it gives them time to plan; to work on their business.

For example, none of you should be doing your own book-keeping – well unless you are a bookkeeper of course – and I'll prove it to you. Let's assume that you are pretty competent at bookkeeping and you spend three hours working on your books. Now however good you are, an experienced book-keeper will do the work faster, and probably better. Let's say they do the work in two hours. So you have already saved an hour. But what about the cost? Obviously different bookkeepers charge varying amounts but the average is currently around £20 per hour. So this job would have cost £40. Now, what's your hourly rate? £50 per hour? Therefore three hours of your work is worth £150. It doesn't need a bookkeeper to work out that you have just lost £110 by doing it yourself. Convinced? You should be. I can safely say that I've never done my own bookkeeping; when I first started my mum did it for me!

The great thing about assistants is that you can employ them by the hour and you can employ different assistants for different jobs. And you don't even need an office for them because today many assistants are virtual (they work from home or their own office). There has never been a better time for you not to be your own assistant.

Okay, so there are jobs in your business that you shouldn't be doing, and that could even be the work that your business does - after all Sir Richard Branson doesn't fly his own planes – but how do you decide? Well the following is something that I get all of my mentees to do; not only does it show them the jobs that they shouldn't be doing, but it also saves them time, and helps to prioritise what they are doing. It makes a big difference to their success but it can be hard to do.

We are going to work on an overall plan here, but it is something that you can do daily and certainly weekly.

Now the first thing you have to do is to imagine that you have staff (if you work on your own) and the second, more difficult thing, is to be brutally honest.

Right you need a sheet of A4 paper (ipad if you must) in front of you, laid down landscape (long ways). You then need to make four equal columns across the page, headed A, B, C and D.

Now this is where it gets difficult; you really need to think.

In column A you list the things that only you can do. Now remember this has nothing to do with numbers of staff. If you do this well column A will be one of your shorter lists. Then in column B you put all the things that it would be good if you did them but, in truth, someone else could do them. And in column C you put all the things that you definitely shouldn't be doing – like bookkeeping. Column D is a tricky one because you have to be honest and admit to something you won't want to. You see column D is for all the things that if they didn't happen no one would notice and they wouldn't make any difference to the success of your business. Trust me, you will have some things in column D.

Then you prioritise the things in each column: one to however many there are; one being the most important.

Now we can get to work. The first thing to do is easy. Anything in column D you forget. You've just said no one would notice if it did happen and it wouldn't make any difference to your business anyway – so it's gone. Time saved already.

Column A is also pretty easy. They are the things that only you can do and you know which of them is the most important; you do that first (before anything). You might not want to do what is top of your list, because it's challenging, but again you have said it is the most important thing you have to do. So do it you must.

Column C just requires you to let go: to understand that you don't have to do everything yourself, shouldn't be doing everything yourself, and that you will achieve a great deal more if you get the right people to help you. This is where you will save an enormous amount of time and have the potential to earn a lot more money. A cautionary note here – there is no point employing someone to do a job if you then waste the time saved. You must put the saved time to good use.

And Column B is the most problematic to sort out and will take some thought, but I think by now you know what you need to do.

In business you will be told that you should be 'working on your business rather than in your business' and this technique will allow you the time to make a start.

# A new member of staff!

If you are a member of an average-sized networking group, one with over thirty members, for a reasonable number of years, you might be surprised at just how many members that group will have had in that time. In my case, as a long-term member (ten years), the number was well over one hundred and fifty.

Now you might be thinking, "Wow, that's bad!" But trust me, it's not. (Well it doesn't have to be.) You see 'fresh blood' can be good for a group as it helps to keep things invigorated. Also groups not only grow, they also shrink; people leave. And although many members see people leaving as a bad thing, a reflection on them and their group, it's not. Well, not in most cases anyway.

You see people's lives are changing all of the time; they leave jobs, move house, get married, get divorced, retire, close a business, move a business, go and travel the world, emigrate, get promoted, the list is virtually endless. And so groups continually grow and shrink, and that's why, just like any other business, a successful networking group always needs visitors. It was on one of these changes of members that I first met Ross. The plumber in my group had left to travel (Australia if I remember correctly), and so the group had a vacancy for a new plumbing company.

Ross is one of the most driven, committed and organised people that I have ever met during my years networking. But what made him extra special was that he wanted to learn everything he could about business. And so it wasn't long before he asked if I would mentor him. As I have already said, Ross was a very capable young man but this was the first time he had run a business, in effect, on his own. What he wanted from me was to benefit from my experience of actually having run my own business, the day-to-day stuff, that's not easily explained in a book, or completely obvious, unless you have already done it.

One of our greatest successes was when Ross wanted to take on his first (senior) member of staff. He says that this one event was worth my total fee all on its own. It was during our third, monthly, session that he announced that he was going to get a new member of staff. And innocently I asked why? His answer was because he needed one. So I repeated my question. Why? And again he replied, because he needed one. And once again I asked, why?

You see all too often business owners employ their first member of staff without actually knowing why they are doing it. They know they are busy and have far too much to do, so they assume that they must need a member of staff. The problem with taking on staff using this method (no clear understanding of why) is that, more often than not, the new employee doesn't understand their role, has very little to do, and gets bored. Whereas the employer is just as busy as ever and thinks their new member of staff is inefficient at best and plain lazy at worst. And this was the reason that I was pushing Ross to think about why he thought he needed a new member of staff.

An hour later we had worked out precisely what this new member of staff would do. But, more importantly, what Ross wouldn't be doing in the future. What's more, we had developed a perfect job spec for the recruitment agency.

The other thing that we considered was what the new employee would need to be taught, what training they could be given and when, and what key attributes the person would need as a pre-requisite of employment. A 'can-do' attitude was top of Ross' list.

What makes this story even more interesting is that I found Ross his new member of staff.

Over the months I had spent a fair amount of time talking to one of the staff at a venue I used. He had a great attitude, nothing was too much trouble for him, and he always had a smile in welcome for all he met. And he wanted to get on. Shortly after having my meeting with Ross (the one about him needing a new member of staff), I used the venue again and got to speak to my contact as usual. It wasn't in my mind to start with, but as we chatted it became clear that he fitted Ross' job description to the letter. So I carefully asked the question, might he be looking for a new job and what did he think about running a plumbing business? His reply was an immediate yes and he would love the opportunity. Well, to cut a long story short, I made the introductions, and eighteen months later my contact was managing the office, allowing Ross to open another site. It was just brilliant and all made possible because I knew exactly what Ross was looking for, and so did he.

Unless you have already done this exercise yourself, I can't recommend you doing it anything like enough, because the benefits can be just staggering. Even if you already have staff, or have no intention of taking any on in the near future, it's more than worthwhile. In fact, even if you are the only person in your business.

As business owners, and employers, we have many different jobs. Of course the big ones are easy to think about: sales, marketing, accounts, invoicing, estimating, stock-ordering and, of course, doing the work. But what about: servicing vehicles, MOTs, ordering stationery, keeping virus software on computers up to date, ensuring the website is current, doing the post, and all the other things that it takes to run a successful business?

Doing this exercise has a number of benefits. If you run your business on your own it will identify the things that you shouldn't be doing (answering the phone and going to the bank for example). If you are looking for staff (as Ross was), it can help you find your ideal member of staff. And if you already have staff you may just discover that there are jobs your staff should be doing and, quite often, that certain jobs should be swapped around your team.

There are also s couple of other things that this exercise frequently shows up. Firstly, there are jobs that no one is responsible for, and that's why often these jobs don't get done. And secondly, there are jobs that everyone seems to be doing, leading to confusion and wasted resources (staff time and money). I'm sure you've heard the "Oh, I've already done that!" comment around the office.

As I say, this is such a wonderful little exercise and it will help you with planning, getting truly organised, and aiding the smooth operation of your company. It will also improve staff morale and customer service. And of course, in turn, this will help your profits. Done properly this exercise can make a massive difference to the way your company performs.

# She's really great!

I was sitting in a networking meeting when the man sitting opposite me got up and said, "Nothing this week, but I would just like to say that Stephanie did a brilliant job for me. She's really great", and sat down again.

It wasn't the most inspiring contribution to a meeting that I had ever witnessed but at least I knew that Stephanie had done a brilliant job. In truth I didn't know exactly what she had done, so the testimonial didn't really help me, or her, that much, but at least I knew she was great.

It certainly wasn't the best of testimonials but better than nothing. The thing is we all love testimonials; in fact, it would be hard to imagine the world without them. Let's face it we've all gone to a restaurant because a friend has recommended it. And it doesn't stop there, it's just the same with; films, holidays, cars, mobiles, tennis coaches, and just about everything else you can think of. So, why is this? Well, it's because we all find endorsements by our fellow consumers (and those we trust - friends) far more convincing than what people trying to sell us stuff actually say about themselves; none of us like taking the risk of being fooled by some clever advertising. It's safer, it gives us permission to buy, and therefore, as a business owner, we really need to understand this and ensure that we are using our own testimonials the very best way we can.

A good testimonial will relate to your prospective customers and will build their trust in you and increase your credibility with them. It will tell them that you can solve their problems and it's safe to spend their hard-earned cash with you.

It is said that between 20% and 50% of buying decisions are influenced by a testimonial and that testimonials increase conversion rates by as much as 25%. And with video testimonials, it's even better, where conversion is increased by a staggering four times that of a written one. Now those figures make it a must for every business owner to use testimonials and to use them well.

So, what makes a good testimonial?

Well going back to my "She's really great" experience, it needs to be rather more than that to be of any real worthwhile benefit.

To begin with the testimonial needs to introduce the person giving it so that others see them as a real person that they can identify with. So, it needs to contain their name, what they do, and what the problem was that they were having.

Then it needs to cover how the problem was solved and finally the benefit. All the time making it real. If someone saved you £39,450, don't say around £40,000. A real figure is so much more believable.

With this in mind a much better testimonial for Stephanie would have sounded something like this:

"My name is David Wimblett and I am the author of the book 'The Ten Year Breakfast', but something that I have to admit is that my English grammar and spelling is not great for a writer and so my draft scripts are littered with mistakes. Luckily I was introduced to Stephanie, who is an exceptional proof reader. She is very precise and, as yet, has never been thrown by some of my odd writings.

This is my second book to be published with her help; something I never thought would have been possible before I met her. And she has helped me to fulfil my dream of having a best seller.

I would just like to say that Stephanie has done a brilliant job for me. She's really great."

I hope that you will agree that a testimonial similar to this would be of far greater benefit to her than one just saying, she is great.

Now this is very important. A testimonial is of little use if no one believes it. Don't know about you but when I just see initials at the end of a testimonial, 'made up', pops into my head; or is that just me? So, at this point you want as much detail about the person as possible: full name, company if there is one, job title, full address, and photo of the person (if possible). The more you can get of these details the more trustworthy the testimonial will be and the more business it will generate for you.

And a few other things to help you.

Collect as many testimonials as you can, make it a regular habit, and make sure you show them off. But please don't have a boring 'Testimonial' page on your website, but instead give the page a more interesting title. More importantly, have testimonials on as many pages of your website as you can. You can add them to the quotes you send out – both written and email – this can make a big difference to conversion. But always make the testimonial relevant. A great testimonial, which talks about tiling, is of little use if the job you are quoting on is building a wooden bookcase.

With video, the secret is for the person speaking to be authentic; it doesn't have to be perfect but it needs to be real. As for length – between thirty seconds and a minute is about right.

One last thing. How do you get those testimonials? Well, I find by far the easiest method is just to ask for them; you will be surprised at just how many people will want to say good things about you.

# Building your list

Ask any successful business owner and they will tell you that their 'list' is their most valuable asset. And by list I mean database of clients, ex-clients and potential clients.

Both Facebook (1.26 billion users) and Twitter (500 million users) are worth a fortune. Why? Because of the size of their databases.

I have to admit that it was some time before I discovered the importance of growing my list and I have to say that I am the poorer for it. But, having learnt of my error, I quickly did something about it and, furthermore, I make sure that all of my clients don't make the same mistake that I did.

However, I have discovered that very few business owners spend any time building a database, even when the opportunity presents itself to them. Because of this they are missing out on thousands of pounds worth of possible business, if not tens of thousands, and, in some cases, hundreds of thousands.

Over the years I have given many 'education slots' to networking groups and one of my favourite such slots is on list building because not only can it make such a big difference to the success of a business but in networking it is very easy to do.

To succeed, a business always needs to be growing; there is no such thing as standing still. So, if your business isn't growing it has to be shrinking, and that's not great. Sooner or later it will mean trouble. So your business must be growing; all of the time.

Well one of the networking groups I worked with (BNI) know their numbers. And they are very simple. Three visitors a week and the group will grow, two visitors a week and they may stay reasonably stable, but with one visitor a week they will be shrinking, and eventually, if nothing changes, simply die. So, obviously, all BNI groups have a target of three visitors each week. This gave me the basis of my education slot.

On average a BNI group has thirty members and the first question of my education slot is, "Who has a record of all of the visitors to the chapter in the last year?" On a good morning, one hand might go up. That means twenty-nine business owners have missed the opportunity to build their client base. Now this is where more numbers come in. Three visitors a week is 150 people a year. That's 150 potential clients. The problem is that way too many business owners are short-sighted. They only think of the business they could do today; even in good networking groups. They don't think about the possible business in the future - maybe a year or more in the future.

I gave this education slot one morning where one of the members of the group had been a member for thirteen years. That amounts to a staggering 1950 people that could be on that member's database. They weren't. Add to that all the other people he would have met networking during that time and we are talking of around 2500 people. Each one he would have met, talked to, and had something in common with, and therefore had a great reason to have kept it touch. What a missed opportunity. Just imagine the business he has missed out on over the years.

Building a good database is vital to the success of a business and there are many ways of doing it, but networking is one of the easiest and most effective because of the relationship between the two parties. But so many of the people that network miss it. Please don't be one of them.

Now I'm usually asked two questions and both are easy to answer. First, how and in what format do I keep this information? Well to start with Excel, or a similar spreadsheet programme, is fine. But long term, you want a good CRM (Customer Relationship Management) system. You can get them for free or of course, spend a good amount of money on a system. When choosing which to buy you need to be clear as to what you want it to do and then ask for recommendations. Don't just go off and buy the first CRM you like the look of. I promise you a good CRM is a must. A few hundred customers on an Excel sheet is one thing, but when you get into the thousands you must be in control. But the big thing about a CRM system is that it is far more than just a database: it's a sales tool and that is where you will really win.

Then the second question is usually, "what do I say to them?" Well again this is easy. Just imagine that you are down the pub – and you've only had the one drink. You wouldn't go into a full scale sales-pitch. Would you? Well, I hope not!

Your first follow-up is a simple; "It was great to meet you. If I can help you in any way. Let's keep in touch". That sort of thing. It's about growing the relationship. You might get a reply by return, if you have sent an email, or you might not hear at all. But either way you can keep in touch. An instant reply is a good sign that the other person is open to continuing the relationship. A meeting over coffee could be the ideal next step. Even with someone who has not replied to you, there is no harm in the occasional contact. After all they may just be busy at that moment in time. The situation may be completely different six months down the road.

The important thing is to keep in touch with the people you meet. And remember – not loads of sales stuff. That's why most people get fed up with communications, because it's just sales, sales, and more sales. Instead, send useful stuff and you will find that people ask for more and look forward to hearing from you. And that is when good things happen.

*Note: Facebook and Twitter numbers correct at the time of writing.*

# Handbags!

I was watching England play rugby at Twickenham (on the television) when there was a bit of a 'set-to' between a couple of the players. One of the players had caught the other with his boot. The referee stepped in, pulled the players apart, and gave them both a ticking-off.

Neither player was booked, but the best part was, now that the officials are 'miked-up', you could hear everything the referee said, and in his opinion it was "...no more than handbags..." I just love that.

In my time networking I have witnessed a number of cases of 'handbags', from just raised voices, to being shouted at in the lobby of The Marriott Hotel at Heathrow (a member didn't agree with what I was enforcing!), to a full scale punch up in a venue car park. And, some very bad language.

On all of those occasions it was 'heat of the moment' reactions to, in truth, 'nothing events'. Sorry if you were one of them and still think otherwise!

But, whatever the event, shouting, handbags, full scale punch-ups, or anything else for that matter (abusive emails) are not the answer to your problems. If you ever have a problem with another member of your networking group, the place to start is with the management team of your group, and always put your grievance in writing. I suggest in writing because that involves sitting down and thinking. The 'heat-of-the-moment' will have passed, and, guess what? When you set about writing, nine times out of ten, you really do see that the problem was a 'nothing event' and won't bother to go any further.

I remember a particular time getting a phone call from one of the more 'colourful' members of the group. He was livid. It took me a full ten minutes before I could calm him down enough and find out exactly what the problem was. In truth I already knew as, at the meeting that morning, I had heard one of the presentations given contain a major cross-over of business in its request.

You see, the problem with single category networking groups is that there is always cross-over between certain types of business. For example, accountants often also offer bookkeeping as a service, but bookkeeping is a separate category. So, an accountant can't talk about bookkeeping in the group. Likewise, a printer will do artwork, but graphic design (which includes artwork) is a separate category. So, the printer can't mention artwork. It can be tricky.

Anyway, back to my irate member. He wanted to make an official complaint, in writing, there and then. He couldn't let this pass. The other member's sales pitch had been all about his area of work. He wanted something done now. Today. He wanted action!

I ventured that I was sure that it had just been a mistake by the member concerned. This sometimes happens as it's not always clear where the cross-over point is between two categories. For example, this cross-over is often a challenge with regard to insurance when an IFA, mortgage broker, and insurance broker are involved, as both an IFA and mortgage broker insure their clients, and an insurance broker can insure everything.

No, he insisted. He wanted to make an official complaint and he wanted me to do something about it. Right then. Ring the member, he demanded.

Wouldn't he like to wait? Give it a day? Things would seem different tomorrow, I said.

No. No. No. He almost shouted. He wanted to act fast and make sure it never happened again. I had to do something.

"How about a coffee?" I suggested. Have a coffee with the member and discuss things. "You must be joking," came his reply.

I tried again. "What harm could a coffee do?"

"Why would I want a coffee with a bloke who's trying to steal my business?" he asked. I said that I was sure that the member wasn't trying to steal his business. I was sure that it was just an innocent mistake. The phone was silent. "Are you sure a coffee is a good idea?" he asked.

"Yes", I said.

"Do you really think so?" he asked again, I assured him that I did.

Finally we agreed that he would ring the member and invite him for a coffee and if that really didn't clear things up I would act on his written complaint.

The next day I received another phone call. They had had a coffee as I suggested. The other member had no idea that there was a problem; that there had been any cross-over at all (interesting in itself). So they had discussed things and decided exactly what each would cover. "Great", I said.

"But, there's more", he said. "We are going to work together on a big project he has coming up as it's too big for his company to handle on its own. It's brilliant."

"And, you didn't want a coffee," I said (bit smart I know). We exchanged a few words of good natured humour and said our goodbyes.

Just before he rang off, he said "Thank you".

Sometimes you just get things right. I have to say that I felt rather happy that day.

As BT says, "It's good to talk", and it's often a good idea to 'count to ten' before you act in the heat of the moment. So, my advice: if you ever have a problem in your networking group, go home, think about it, and then talk. It's amazing what can be achieved with a clear head, over a cup of coffee.

# I run for charity

In 1999 I was recommended to the NBFA, a charity that assists the elderly, as a printer who knew what he was talking about. Isn't it great when you get a testimonial like that?

So, a few days later I found myself sitting in the London office of the CEO and she explained some of the problems that they were having with their current printer. One was the quality of what they produced and she showed me a Christmas card they had printed for them. I didn't say so, but I had rarely seen such poor printing, and assured her that our print would be better; in fact way better.

But it was her next question that really 'got' me. She explained that every year they would use one, maybe two, of the original paintings they owned, sometimes very valuable paintings, as artwork for their Christmas cards. I said that was fine. But, as I say it was her question that surprised me. She asked if they would get the paintings returned. I replied, "Of course!" It seemed their current printer wouldn't guarantee their return and, even if they did return them, then they may be damaged. I think she saw the shock on my face, at the thought of not returning her paintings, and the account was mine. Furthermore, not only did the NBFA get better Christmas cards and their paintings returned, without a scratch, I also saved them money. Overall a great result.

As our relationship grew I became more involved in the process of choosing which cards to print and became part of the panel that decided on which cards to print and how many to order. This led to advising on other areas of print and then into brain-storming ideas for fund-raising.

It was at one of these brain-storming sessions that I suggested the idea of the NBFA organising their own 5k Fun Run. Not only would it raise funds, but it would also raise their profile and be great PR. They thought it a great idea and asked if I would run it. I couldn't really say no as it was my idea and agreed. Again I got the job, but to my surprise it wasn't the job I thought I was agreeing to (again I didn't say this). It only became clear a few minutes later that they weren't asking if I would run in the 5k, they were asking if I would organise the whole event for them.

I have always enjoyed a challenge, and having recovered from the shock of what I had agreed to, left promising a proposal in a few days' time.

Now at this stage all I knew about 5k Fun Runs was what I had learnt from having completed a few. But how hard could it be?

I decided that organisation was the key. And I reasoned that as I had run a successful company for many years, if nothing else I could certainly organise a well-run event. So, where to begin?

I think my decision on where to begin was the reason that the events were so successful (I didn't stop at one). It occurred to me that a running event was no different to a customer ordering print and so I decided to start with the runner. What made a good event for them? At the time one of my sons was training for the London Marathon (I was his trainer) and he was taking part in a lot of races. Obviously, as his coach, I went with him to all of his races and this meant a lot of, to be honest, hanging around. But now I had a purpose; I studied every single thing that happened at each event: from the initial entry booking, to any after-event communication; what was good from a runner's perspective and what was not. And I learnt a great deal.

I now needed 3 things: a lot of help, a lot of stuff, and a lot of runners!

And this is where I have to say a great big thank you to all my friends and contacts that I've met at network events over the years; plus my wife, four sons, and two of their girlfriends.

Almost everything for the event came from my network. From design of leaflets, the race numbers (my best friend claimed number one), to prizes, the Goody bags, 500 bottles of water, traffic cones, a time-keeper (volunteer from the Bushy Park 5k), marshals, car park security, personal trainer, physio and a man to lead the runner round the course on his bicycle. And of course a lot of runners and fund raisers.

BNI members accounted for nearly half of the runners that first year, including the joint National Directors Charlie Lawson and Tim Cook. And over the next few years two chapters, Business Class and Tudor, had quite a tussle as to who were the best overall team. It's still hotly contested today!

The events raised a lot of money for the NBFA and was fun to organise and I even got to take part in a race myself one year.

Without my network I don't think it would have been possible to organise the Fun Runs for the NBFA, I certainly know that it would have been a great deal harder. And I guess that's my point. Networking is not just about business, it's about how well you know someone, and what you will do for that person. I have made some wonderful friends networking over the years and we have done a great deal of business together.

So, I guess my message here is build great long term relationships with people and business will just follow, because, as I've said before, we like doing business with people we like. But what's more important is that we go out of our way to help our friends and the NBFA 5k Fun Runs were the perfect example of this.

# Keep it simple!

Often we complicate things for no apparent reason. I'm not exactly sure why, we just do. Perhaps it's to show how clever we are, maybe it's to prove our worth, or possibly it's because we just can't believe that something simple can be any good. Maybe it's because we just don't think.

There's a joke, I expect you've heard, that when the American's went into space they needed a pen that would write upside down and they spent millions perfecting a ballpoint pen that would do the job. Whereas, faced with the same problem, the Russians gave their astronauts a pencil (it's worth looking up the real story). But, true or not, it does make my point for me. Over the years I've been lucky enough to visit a numbers of countries to give talks on networking and referrals.

I've already mentioned my visit to Japan, but I've also been to Ireland, Scotland and Africa. Kenya wasn't precisely planned but nicely demonstrates the power of international networks. The trip to Kenya also involved stopping off in Uganda on the way. We were visiting a school in Uganda which was twinned with a school local to where I live. This UK school had raised some funds to buy a generator for the school in Uganda but didn't want to just hand over the money. With my contacts in Kenya I was able to locate a reliable contractor who could supply the generator and the deal was done.

Then in Kenya we visited a charity, near Meru, for one of the members of my own network. They raised funds for the charity, in both the UK and Australia. Both wonderful things to be able to do.

Whilst we were in Nairobi, I discovered that there was a (morning) networking meeting in our hotel. So I found myself, on my birthday, doing an Education Slot at the launch meeting of a new group. I have to say that it was very special. But I think Scotland was where I had the most fun. I went there for two days each month for a number of months: mentoring, training, attending management meetings and, of course, giving Education Slots.

There were a number of reasons as to why my trips were always great fun but one has to be a guy called Colin Read (now Executive Director of BNI in Scotland South & East). His sense of fun is contagious and he gives the most entertaining but also practical and useful workshops. I remember two of his workshops in particular. One where he ran onto the stage leapt onto a chair and the lifted his kilt, to reveal a message written on his thigh. It certainly got everyone's attention! In my own case, because if he thought I was going to give this

Education Slot, with my skinny little thighs, he had another thought coming! There was another time when he had a large group of us stand in a circle. Once in the circle we then all had to sit on the lap of the person behind us. Everyone had to do it, at the same time, or we would fall over. It was a brilliant way to demonstrate what can be done if people work as a team.

In comparison my ideas were very modest, nowhere as much fun, but thankfully just as successful.

Something that I had discovered during my time with my referral group was that I had a knack for getting other business people to come to our meetings. One year I managed to entice forty-three visitors along to my group. Now people thought I was an incredible visitor finder, and, I guess, in some ways I was, but I didn't have and special talents. No special gift. I just did what all successful businesses do, because finding visitors for a group is no different to finding new customers, I marketed my group in as many ways as possible, and I did it consistently. Never did a week go by that I didn't invite someone, somehow, along to my group (even when on holiday!).

One of the ways that I invite people is by using a postcard. I have something of a reputation for it.

The principle is very simple and, oh, so easy to implement. My goal was to give out two postcards a week. Just two. There's not a person who networks who couldn't do this if they truly wanted to. It can be very targeted because I decided who I gave the cards to, or a little more random (anyone, anywhere), but it worked. As I say, it was both simple and easy to do, but as with all things that are simple and easy, they still have to be done, and done correctly.

This is how my system worked. I always carried two postcards in my jacket pocket (ladies can have them in their handbags) and they were written out with the detail of my next meeting. Why? Well, for two reasons. One, it made sure I gave them out. And two, because often you don't have the time to write out the details on a card when you meet someone. Especially when using one of my techniques for distributing them!

And this is the method that I'm famous for: the garage forecourt.

When we fill our cars with fuel we are stuck for a couple of minutes at the fuel filler. If a car pulls up opposite you can either stare into space or intently study the numbers on the dials telling us how much fuel is being poured into the tank. Sometimes a woman might get a smile out of me.

But if a tradesman's, sign-written van, pulled up beside me I swung into action. First, I would give the person a knowing nod. Then I would ask how business was and usually got an 'okay' for my trouble. Next I would ask if they were looking for any more work and the answer was always 'yes'. Then I would pounce. My postcard came out of my pocket in a nanosecond and was handed to my unsuspecting victim. It's amazing how hard it is to refuse something when it's handed to you. You take it, it's just a reflex action. As the person took the card I would say, "Then this might be of interest to you. If you want to know more just give me a call. My number's on the card." Job done.

Now you might be thinking, well that doesn't sound like very target marketing. But you would be wrong. For one thing I would only engage with local tradesman, but more than that, I would only give the cards to tradesman not already represented in my group. Plus these people were looking for more work. I think that's pretty targeted.

Well, it was on one of my visits to Scotland that Colin asked me to talk about 'My Postcards' at one of his workshops. I have to say the idea went down a storm and people couldn't believe how simple the idea was. What's more they all committed to giving it a try. The marvellous thing is that the cards are still bringing in results today.

But as I said earlier you do have to follow all of the stages of a system for the best effect, as one pretty young lady, in one of Colin's groups, discovered. She was going out for the evening, clubbing I think it was, and had to stop for petrol. As she filling her car a BMW pulled up in the next bay. Being a keen member she had her two postcards in her handbag and sprang into action. A well-dressed man climbed out of the car and as he did so she said, "You looking for business?" The man, clearly shocked, took one look at the glamorous young lady asking the question and jumped back into his car and sped off. Leaving our young lady somewhat bemused. I promise you this is a true story and just demonstrates how important it is to be careful if you miss out any steps of a plan that works.

There's another story from Scotland which shows how a simple incentive can work. Again it concerns postcards. One of Colin's groups holds a weekly draw. A bottle of wine is the prize –

that's all. To take part in the draw you have to bring in a postcard. The postcards go into a hat and the winner is drawn out. That's it. Bring in five postcards and you have five chances of winning the bottle. So simple. Every week the group gets between twenty and thirty postcards handed in. There is one condition in order to qualify for the draw. The postcard must be targeted; it must be addressed to a named person.

# An Offer from David

for readers of The 10 Year Breakfast.

Thank you for reading my book. I hope you've found it not only interesting and useful but also a bit of fun; and most importantly of real value.

Now at this point we can either go our separate ways or stay in touch and as you have taken the time to read my book I'd really like for us to stay in touch.

So I have a FREE GIFT for you – a copy of my 'Business Bites' CD.

Business Bites is an audio CD which covers, in around 40 minutes, three or four essential topics which when implemented in your business will make a massive difference to your success.

Simply go to:
http://www.7training.co.uk/businessbites.html
or email:
businessbites@7training.co.uk (Subject: Free Business Bites CD)

I hope that you will accept my gift but should you decide not to I wish you well on your business journey.

*Offer is subject to change without notice.*

# Index